Fox Terrier

You are holding a reproduction of an original work that is in the public domain in the United States of America, and possibly other countries.You may freely copy and distribute this work as no entity (individual or corporate) has a copyright on the body of the work.This book may contain prior copyright references, and library stamps (as most of these works were scanned from library copies).These have been scanned and retained as part of the historical artifact.

This book may have occasional imperfections such as missing or blurred pages, poor pictures, errant marks, etc. that were either part of the original artifact, or were introduced by the scanning process. We believe this work is culturally important, and despite the imperfections, have elected to bring it back into print as part of our continuing commitment to the preservation of printed works worldwide. We appreciate your understanding of the imperfections in the preservation process, and hope you enjoy this valuable book.

From a painting by Arthur Wardle.
Ch. Donna Fortuna
Smooth-haired Fox Terrier by Ch. Dominie ex Ch. Dame Fortune

From a painting by W. Watts, A. R. S. A.
Ch. Dusky Reine
Wire-haired Fox Terrier by Ch. Royston Remus ex Don't Go

THE FOX TERRIER

BY
WILLIAMS HAYNES

Author of "The Airedale," "Scottish and Irish Terriers," "The Bull Terrier," etc.

NEW YORK
OUTING PUBLISHING COMPANY
MCMXII

Copyright, 1912, by
OUTING PUBLISHING COMPANY

All rights reserved

CONTENTS

CHAPTER	PAGE
I. THE BEST KNOWN TERRIER	1
II. THE SMOOTH FOX TERRIER	21
III. THE WIRE-HAIRED FOX TERRIER	39
IV. THE TERRIER'S EDUCATION	53
V. TERRIERS IN HEALTH	63
VI. DISEASES AND REMEDIES	77
VII. THE SCIENCE OF DOG BREEDING	93
VIII. SHOWS AND SHOW DOGS	109

THE BEST KNOWN TERRIER

CHAPTER I

THE BEST KNOWN TERRIER

"DOGS may come, and dogs may go; but the Fox Terrier goes on forever," is a doggy proverb that is literally true. In spite of all the whims of fickle Mistress Fashion and in the face of the keenest competition from all sorts and conditions of canine novelties, the Fox Terrier always remains—with the general public at least—the best known of all terriers.

Over in England, the land of his birth, he is and long has been the most popular of dogs. The Bulldog sets up to be Britain's "national breed;" but the Fox Terrier makes his claims rather fanciful, for he greatly outnumbers the popular dog with the smashed-in face and the bow legs. Moreover, he is a terrier, and the terriers are distinctively British in origin, while the bulldog is a member of the mastiff family, which if not imported by the Normans, was at least crossed extensively with big, heavy dogs from the Continent.

THE FOX TERRIER

With the Atlantic Ocean and more than a hundred and thirty five Fourth-of-Julys between us, this is not a discussion over which we American dog fanciers are going to lose very much sleep, but it is good to know that this terrier is not without honor in his own country. In England, in "the Colonies," or in Timbuctoo, an Englishman and his Fox Terrier are almost as inseparable as an Englishman and his pipe.

In America the dog is certainly the best known of the terriers. Scores upon scores of people who could not tell an Airedale from a Scottie if their lives depended on it, and hundreds who have never even heard of a Bedlington or a Dandie Dinmont, know—or think they know—a Fox Terrier.

The whole country is overrun with so-called Fox Terriers, unauthorized editions that bear but scant resemblance to the original. Not one in a thousand among them has anything that their most enthusiastic and imaginative friend could call a pedigree, but originally they must have been mainly Fox Terrier in blood and they still (more's the pity!) boast the proud name of the race to which they can claim such slight relationship.

They are Fox Terriers run wild and gone to seed. They are as full of faults as an alley cur is of fleas. Their heads are short, thick in skull, and snippy in muzzle. They always have crazy ears—either big, pendulous affairs like a hound, or else small and pricked like a Pomeranian, with sometimes a little variety introduced in the form of neatly turned "rose ears" so ardently desired by the breeder of bulldogs. They have shockingly bad fronts, with straight, heavy shoulders and pipe-stem legs.

The real Fox Terrier is a very different looking dog. He is quite the elegant among terriers; a clean thoroughbred showing his breeding in every line and movement. His white jacket, with its irregular splashes of color —usually black, more rarely a pretty tan— catches any eye. His good looks can be appreciated at a glance by the uninitiated, while it often requires a pretty thorough education in canine loveliness to see the beauty in some other breeds.

The head of the modern thoroughbred is long, with a flat skull, clean cheeks, and a strong muzzle. It is certainly suggestive of a long, blunt-pointed wedge, though not so wedgy as the Bull Terrier's head. The ears should be V-shaped and buttoned over forward. They must be small and thin, but not too much so, or they will look light and flippy. They are to be set on the angle of the corner of the skull, not up on the top, nor down behind the cheeks. A small, dark eye, full of fire, is essential to the correct expression. The teeth, which are just covered with tight lips, must be strong, level, and white. The proper nose is black, and the nostrils are quite large.

This head sets on a longish neck that curves into the line of the back and sweeps down into the chest. The throat is clean, and the chest narrow but deep. Many of the dogs of to-day are shallow chested, which does not make for sound "bellows and pump," and others are too narrow, a fault that is usually accompanied by tied in elbows and turned out toes. The shoulder of a race horse, long, clean, sloping, muscular without being heavy, is the shoulder desired. The forelegs should be straight as strings, and the bone of even thickness all the way down. The correct elbows are turned neither in nor out. The pasterns must be springy, but strong.

Short and level describes the Fox Terrier's back. His brisket must be deep and well ribbed up, but a balloon roundness is quite as bad as slab-sided flatness. His loin should be slightly cut up—not enough to give him a wasp waist, but sufficient to remove any suggestion of a sausage body.

Some of the Fox Terriers we see are decidedly light in the hindquarters. These should be strong. The thighs must be muscular, with hocks that set down near the ground. These hocks must be strong and straight, making a perpendicular line to the level of the earth.

The tail ought to be carried gaily, almost at right angles with the back, but it is a fault if it curls over farther than this. A "cat foot," small, compact, and well knuckled up, is the foot that will carry him to first prizes.

Color and markings are not of the most vital importance, for a good one cannot be a bad color, as the saying is. All that is required is that the white shall predominate (so that the black, or black and tan, or tan shall be marks) and that there shall not be any liver or brindle coloring.

As all know, there are two kinds of coats for a Fox Terrier, the smooth and the wire. On these the two different varieties are founded, both being judged by the same Standard, except for their coats. The smooth division must have jackets that are thick, rather coarse, and while longer than a Bull Terrier still must be short enough to be a really smooth coat. The wire jacket is longer, like bristles, straight and without any inclination to curl. Under the wire coat, except on the head and legs, is a soft under-jacket.

I am afraid that this description of the perfect Fox Terrier is not very intelligible to one who knows nothing at all of dogs. The collection of the more or less isolated details, bristling with technical jargon, will not, I fear, convey much more idea of how the dog should look than a wall covered with hieroglyphics.

It does not help matters very much to say that a Fox Terrier is a bright, active, cleanly built dog of some eighteen or twenty pounds. He is all that, but he is more. It is a case where ink and paper fail dismally, and to know the real Fox Terrier one must meet him not between the covers of a book, but in the show ring. The inquiring novice will find many willing schoolmasters, for dog fanciers are chummy and not a bit stingy with their doggy knowledge.

We have all met people, who are quite rational beings in other respects, but who claim (and will offer to prove it, too) that a cur is more clever and blessed with a better disposition than a thoroughbred. They will grudgingly grant that the real dog is better looking; "but," they say, "he has not the brains." This is the main prop of those remarkable "Fox Terriers" we meet on the street.

It is difficult to follow their reasonings.

Time and again it has been proved that "blood will tell." A pen of Leghorns or Orpingtons will produce twice as many eggs in a year as the same number of barnyard chickens. Nobody would expect a cold blooded horse to run with a thoroughbred or a hunter; to road with a trotter or a pacer; to draw as much as a Shire or a Percheron. Even Mr. Selfmade is highly tickled to find he can wear a bit of ribbon that signifies not that he has invented a new machine, or engineered a corner, or built up a trust; but that his several times great grandfather fought redskins or redcoats.

The thoroughbred terrier, who for generations has been carefully mated, carefully reared, carefully trained, has miles of handicap over the gutter pup. Some breeds have degenerated into silly monstrosities, lacking in health and in brains, but not so the Fox Terrier, or for that matter, any of the terriers. They are all sound in constitution, and they have that greatest blessing of good breeding in man or beast, the right instincts. They are gentlemen sportsmen—at home in the drawing room, but delighting in the field. This has been the secret of the unrivalled position they hold as the ideal companion.

Accepting the rather transparent fact that the true Fox Terrier is better looking than his doubtful imitation, there are but two rather flimsy excuses for anyone preferring the mongrel: a fictitious quickness of wit and a lower cost. The thoroughbred, as all who know him testify, is more intelligent, more game, and more faithful than his *bourgeois* namesake. "The proof of the pudding is in the eating," and no one who has ever really known the real dog well would keep one of the common counterfeits. As to costs; a Fox Terrier of parts and breeding is not a very expensive investment. A nice puppy can be bought for twenty-five dollars—not, of course, one that will cover your sideboard with cups won at the bench shows, but a real dog, with a real pedigree, and enough of the looks of his parents so that you will not have to apologize whenever a friend who knows something about dogs comes to the house.

With all of his advantages in appearance and disposition, the real Fox Terrier is not commonly popular. Were he more "fancied," his position would be greatly strengthened, for the dog shows are the fashion plates that set the dog styles.

At first glance it is hard to understand how the bench show cult could fail to wax enthusiastic over the dog. He has all the good health and winning disposition that make the terriers proverbially good pals. He is certainly good to look at. Either the wire or the smooth jacket fancier can be satisfied, for the Fox Terrier comes in both varieties of coat. In fact, there is no very obvious reason why they should not be as popular as the other terriers; and their age, backed by their English popularity, should count heavily in their favor. At least so it would seem, but we all know that this is not the case.

The usual explanation is that all the interest has been sucked out of Fox Terriers because two or three big, strong, wealthy kennels have a monopoly of the distribution of show ring honors. As far as it goes, this is a perfectly good explanation. Almost as long as we have had bench shows, the big kennels have carried home the lion's share of the blue ribbons. We have become so used to this state of affairs that we have come to accept a mere statement of this familiar fact as explanation of the dyed-in-the wool fancier's lack of interest in Fox Terriers. We know the breed has suffered because of the strength of a few kennels, but why has it been possible to maintain the monopoly?

The Fox Terrier is very popular in England. He is not very popular in America. These two facts taken together are the reason for the "trust" a few kennels enjoy in our show rings. As a Fox Terrier is a Fox Terrier, be he on this or the other side of the Atlantic, the whole matter is one that rests upon the differences in American and English fanciers.

The Englishman of to-day learned to love the Fox Terrier when a schoolboy. He has remained true to his early love and is not easily weaned away by a novelty. Moreover, the average Englishman demands that his terrier shall be a thoroughbred in breeding, in looks, and in manners. He is not satisfied with a mere dog. There is, as a result, a natural and constant demand for well bred Fox Terriers. This demand is supplied by a great number of Fox Terrier breeders. Many breeders mean many good dogs, and the competition is keen. It is a known fact that a good Fox Terrier is worth more in England than in America, and in no breed will the classes bring together such an even collection of high qualitied specimens.

On the other hand, the average American has not yet learned that a mere dog is not good enough for a pal, or at least, is not as good as a thoroughbred. The comparatively few who do demand good breeding and good looks in their house dogs have rushed after less common dogs than the Fox Terrier. There has not been a demand for well bred Fox Terriers, since the common or garden variety has satisfied the average person.

A really high class dog costs a pretty price in England, and the English kennels were always able to send over one just a little better than the last importation. This, before we had much good breeding stock in the country, made showing Fox Terriers a rich man's game. In this way the monopoly was fostered. The small fancier had neither the incentive of show honors (since a better one than his best could always be imported) nor the expectation of selling his puppies (because those who would pay for a good dog took up other terriers) to encourage him to go in for Fox Terriers.

Will the breed come to its own? The question is obvious and the answer is easy. Certainly, they will. The fact that they are the most generally popular of all the terriers in the land where the terriers were born is pregnant with meaning. The Britisher's love for the breed is guarantee that they have those qualifications that we demand in a terrier. The general public is gradually awakening to the many advantages that the thoroughbred possesses over the mongrel, and in time the run-to-seed " Fox Terriers " will no longer satisfy. If only the dog catcher, or some other benevolent power, would rid the streets of the imitation dogs and their owners should take up the original, the Fox Terrier would make the Boston and Airedale seem insignificant. This is not to be done in a day, but it is coming about gradually.

We are blessed with plenty of breeding stock and our American bred dogs are often real "out and outers." We cannot compete with England in numbers, but for several years we have successively turned out one or two who are of the quality that in several cases could take the measure of the best that the year produced on the other side.

The owners of our big kennels have brought the American breed to a high state of perfection, and even if they have maintained a monopoly, it has been a natural and not a wilful one. Conditions quite beyond control forced the small owners out, and the big owners have done much to keep the dog alive during the lean years when public interest was at low ebb. With the surely increasing number of Fox Terriers devotees, their grip on the prize lists is being gradually lessened, but their well beloved dog is getting stronger and stronger. More power to him!

THE SMOOTH FOX TERRIER

CHAPTER II

THE SMOOTH FOX TERRIER

ONE cool summer evening several years ago, I was sitting in a snug little English cottage listening to an old Fox Terrierite, a man who has been the power behind the throne in several famous kennels, tell anecdotes about past celebrities, both canine and human. Once or twice, the name of a dog would slip away from him. Each time this happened, he would be mightily embarassed, for it touched his pride; and he would say apologetically, "You see, sir, there's been so many good 'uns, they're like the Smiths." He was quite right, and the more one delves into the Fox Terrier's voluminous records, the easier writing a geneology of the Smith family seems to be.

Although far from the most ancient of breeds, this lack of age is easily made up by the wealth of material. The overwhelming popularity of the variety has naturally resulted in so many great show cracks and so many famous strains that anything like a complete history of the Fox Terrier would be a book of enormous bulk. It is both interesting and useful, however, for a fancier to know something of the history of the various breeds—especially the one which he is breeding and exhibiting—and while space does not allow a full and complete record, still we can sketch the more important developments in the evolution of the smooth Fox Terrier.

The best authorities differ considerably on their theories of the breed's origin. On the other hand, those unfamiliar with terrier lore usually hold the belief that the Fox Terrier is the original member of the terrier family. Nothing could be further from the truth. The original terrier stock was wire, not smooth coated, and was black and tan in England and grizzle or reddish in the Border Counties and Lowlands.

The original short coated terrier was the black and tan Manchester Terrier, or at least, his short headed, more chubby ancestors. He antedates the smooth Fox Terrier many years, and indeed, was a factor in his creation.

Every once in a while we come upon reference to a white terrier similar to the black and tan one; but we read of him only in comparatively recent books and we do not see him in sporting paintings or engravings of a century or more ago. Of course, there is the old White English Terrier; but he is a different story, and we know that he came later and from a Whippet cross. I have a suspicion that some Fox Terrier historians have worked from to-day backwards and invented this white smooth dog to account for the Fox Terrier we know. Certainly, white plus black and tan terriers of smooth jackets is a very simple and alluring explanation for the origin of the smooth Fox Terrier. Its very simplicity is against it, for we do not usually find that new breeds are made by the simple addition of one and one.

The earliest record that we have of any white terrier with black markings is a dog called Pitch, owned about 1790 by Colonel Thornton. An engraving by Scott after an oil by Gilpin, which was probably painted from life, was published before 1810 with the following text: " It would be necessary to notice Colonel Thornton's terriers if it were only on account of his justly celebrated Pitch, from whom are descended most of the white terriers in the Kingdom." Judging from this portrait, Pitch was about as near to fifty per cent. Greyhound as a dog could be. He was a big, leggy dog, light in bone, with a longish back and considerable cut up. He seems to have had a nice head—much more the head of to-day than some of the dogs of half a century after him—with small, prick ears. If he were really the dog from whom "most of the white terriers in the Kingdom" came—and this is possible for he would probably be well advertised by his owner's sporting dogs and horses which were greatly sought by wise breeders throughout England—we can be pretty positive in the assertion that the Greyhound was an important contributor in the making of the Fox Terrier.

The Bulldog and the Beagle are also supposed to have been used by early breeders. If the Bulldog has had anything to do with it, I am of the opinion that it was through the Bull Terrier. Such cross breeding could hardly have been done till after 1800, when the Bull Terrier first appeared.

Between Pitch and the middle of the last century is a mysterious gap in Fox Terrier history. We have some bits of broken records and plenty of rumors and traditions, but until 1860, when we can take up the thread and bring it down to to-day without a break, there is not much that is definite. How very shaky the foundation for a pure bred strain was even in the sixties is shown by the fact that some of the illustrious dogs of that day had one black and tan parent, and some were half Bull Terrier, and half Pointer, and one is recorded as having had a Dalmatian dam.

From 1870 till now, we have, as I have said, a complete and perfect pedigree for the Fox Terrier. Three dogs, each famous, are the sources from which most modern strains have come. They were old Jock, Old Trap, and Old Tartar.

Old Jock was more on the style of the dog of now than most of his contemporaries. He was a clean, elegant dog. Not of course, anything like so long headed, so straight in front or so racy in outline as a winner of this generation; but more on the modern style. He was out of Grove Pepper (a black and tan bitch) and was sired by Jock, the property of Capt. Percy Williams. Old Tartar, who was founder of the strain made famous by that prince of sporting clergymen, the late "Jack" Russell, was a more compact, thicker set dog who passed on to his sons and daughters his cobby type and his almost vicious gameness. It is supposed that there was more than a suggestion of Bulldog or Bull Terrier in his make-up, especially as brindle markings sometimes cropped out in this strain. Old Trap was from Oakley Hunt. His exact pedigree is disputed but there is a tradition to the effect that he came of a black and tan family.

Among the "ladies" of those early days, one stands out head and shoulders above her rivals. Grove Nettle is a sort of Fox Terrier Mother Eve, and most pedigrees traced back far enough will contain her name several times. In the Stud Book she is registered as by Grove Tartar ex Sting; but I have heard her pedigree given as by a dog called Snap or Snip, owned by J. B. Hodgson, M. F. H., out of Gimlet, by Grove Tartar ex Cambridge Vic.

Following this quartette, came the ever illustrious Belvoir Joe. He was bred by the huntsman of Belvoir, Will Cooper, who mated his Trinket (a very pretty bitch by Trap, owned by the Belvoir earth stopper, ex Ben Morgan's Nettle) to Trimmer, a dog of the famous Grove strain. Belvoir Joe was famous as a show specimen, as a workman, and as a sire.

Belvoir Joe's best son was Belgrave Joe, bred by Mr. Luke Turner. He was a nailing terrier and the daddy of many a good one. Ch. Spice was, in turn, his best get; but he was not so good as his rival Ch. Result, a classic little dog who is generally acknowledged to be one of the great terriers of all time. He was by Roysterer, a dog bred from Mr. Gibson's famous Brockenhurst strain. Ch. Buffer had a son called Buff who deserves special mention as being the originator of the excellent legs and feet that the breed now boasts. Till his time, legs and feet had not been anything to cheer about, but he had fine, heavy bone carried right down to his small, well knuckled feet, and he transmitted this desirable style of underpinning.

And now we have come to the time where we can no longer mention the celebrities individually, for they came in such numbers that even a list of their names would fill page upon page. We can, however, briefly sketch the development of the breed through the various changes of styles.

The early terrier was short coupled, short of leg, and his skull was broader across the top. He was "a brick with the corners knocked off." He was a chunky little cob, while the dog of to-day is built on the lines of a thoroughbred. It is quite customary to lay the blame of this transformation (if blame is the correct word) onto the shoulders of the fox hunting men. In the old days, he was really a *Fox* Terrier, and some of the best dogs and the most useful strains were those that were developed right in the same kennels with various Foxhound packs. At that time, the terriers were actually used in the hunt. The only requirements were enough speed to be on hand when the fox was to be routed out of his den, enough courage to do the job, all squeezed down into a dog small enough to negotiate successfully an eight inch drain, which was the standard size. There was not so much attention paid to physical attractions, though naturally men who valued looks in the horses and hounds would, other things being equal, want as good looking a terrier as possible.

In time, the pace became too swift for the chunky, little terrier. Throughbred blood was introduced into the hunters and the hounds were bred more and more for speed. Fox Terrier breeders followed suit. They quickly developed a long, lank wastrel, with speed enough for short dashes, but lacking in staying powers and so big that he could no more go to earth with Br'er Fox than he could fly. This huge monstrosity had quite a flight in the show ring, but in the hunting field his career was short and sweet. Nowadays, the hunt has changed to a mere excuse to ride cross country. It is not a real fox hunt, but a wild dash over fences and fallows. The Fox Terrier has lost his original job.

Fox Terrier breeders have gradually come back to a reasonably sized dog—not the chunky type of the early days, but a much more sensible and symmetrical animal than the giants of a couple of decades back. The dog built on the thoroughbred lines, with his long head, his clean shoulders, his short back, and his splendid legs and feet is a perfect gem. A good Fox Terrier—and we see any number of them at the shows—is just about the acme of beauty and symmetry.

Of course, there have been those who have raised a howl about the supposed lack of gameness and stamina in the modern dog. Granted that few Fox Terriers to-day are ever called upon to rout out a fox. Granted that a man is not very prone to risk two hundred or more dollars worth of terrier to prove that he is game. But granting these things is not any acknowledgment of lack of willingness or ability on the part of the dog. In fact, we often hear of the less favored brothers and sisters of bench champions who have displayed all the proverbial spunk and spirit of the old time heroes. Those who have had Fox Terriers on a country place and given them the opportunity to make good on vermin, all give them the highest recommendations.

To turn now to the smooth Fox Terrier in America: we are again confronted by more material than space, but I will tell something of the rise of the various leading kennels.

The oldest of our great kennels which has had a continuous history is the Warren, started before 1880 by Messers Lewis and Winthrop Rutherfurd, and carried on since the unfortunate death of the former by the younger brother. Three cracks of the early days of these kennels were Active, Chance, and Tussle—all winners in the eighties. Their first good homebred was Joker who came out in 1882. He was by Nailer, a son of the good-legged Buff, out of Active. Since the days of this Joker, the Warren Kennels have seldom been without a stormer of their own breeding, and I believe that I am correct in saying that Mr. Rutherfurd has won the cup at New York for the best team of four with a quartette of his own breeding and that he is the only fancier who has this great honor. Bowstring and Royal were two other winners of the early days of these kennels.

It was in 1886 that the first real boom took place. Mr. August Belmont and Mr. John E. Thayer had both been active in importing and they had strong strings. The Rutherfurds were on deck and the late Edward Kelley was always to be counted on to show a good one or two. Mr. Belmont had the all white dog Lucifer, a very taking sort of terrier, though light in eye and weak in muzzle. Bacchanal was another of his—a very even terrier barring his legs and feet. Of bitches he had two very good ones in Diadem and Marguerite. A little later he had Safety, a larger bitch and not so good, but more than useful when a team of four was to be made up. Mr. Thayer had the imported Richmond Olive, the best bitch of the day and probably the best Fox Terrier seen in this country up to that time. She weighed about eighteen pounds—which was larger than the average run in her day—and was a beautifully built one, her worst fault being her rather indifferent spirit. Two other good bitches in the Thayer string were Belgrave Primrose, bought from the Warren Kennels, and Richmond Dazzle, one of George Raper's breeding who was imported in 1887. Best of his dogs was Raby Mixer, a shelly type of dog for this time, but one whose head was not to be overlooked.

The Messrs. Rutherfurd had Splauger who did considerable winning, Cornwall Duchess, a tiny lady of under fourteen pounds but full of quality and terrier fire, and their American bred Lady Warren Mixture, bred by the late W. T. McAlees, sired by Mr. Thayer's dog out of a Warren bitch.

Mr. Kelley brought over the famous Spice, but he was long since past his prime when he landed on our shores and he died a year or so after his importation. This fancier then got a son of the old dog; Earl Leycester, not a wonderfully high class dog though decidedly taking in the ring.

In the late eighties, there were no end of importations—it being a sort of game at which the last dog over was apt to be the first in the prize list. This was the more remarkable for there was the greatest kind of variation in type; but this was the uncertain transition period during which the style of terrier we now know was developed. Mr. Belmont brought over Dusky Trap, The Rutherfurds had Raffle, and Mr. Thayer, Dona—to mention the best in each of the leading strings in the early nineties. The best of the American breds was Mr. Belmont's Blemton Victor II, by Dusky Trap ex Verdict. A year or so after this, Warren Safeguard, a dog who won at New York in 1895, came over. He was a big winner and sired a lot of more than useful ones for his austere purchasers. It was about this time too, that Mr. Thayer dropped out of the game.

Mr. George H. Gooderham of Toronto, with the aid of "Charlie" Lyndon, his kennel manager, began to make things interesting with his famous string of Norfolks. His famous Veracity and Handicraft cleaned up things in approved style, and there was always a string of Norfolks to see to it that the lion's share of the honors went over to Canada. Claude Duval, a beautiful dog, clean cut, and sound, came over in 1899, but was beaten for the best in the show by Handicraft, who reigned supreme as the best bitch in America, till the debut of her home bred kennel mate Norfolk Dark Blue, the best one ever bred by the Canadian fancier.

In 1901, Mr. F. H. Farwell made his first entry at New York with a Norfolk dog called Victorious. He did not, however, live up to his name being past his prime, and his ambitious owner, after a couple of equally disastrous purchases, commissioned George Thomas to get together the makings of the now famous Sabine Kennels. In 1903, he had the great Sabine Result, recently imported, who was beaten by Norfolk Parader. This was not as it should have been, for Result was a glorious dog and he proved invaluable at stud, siring half a dozen or more champions. An early bitch of quality was Sabine Lavender. The Toronto fancier dropping out after this, the Texas kennels have been fighting it out with the Warrens, both of them showing home breds.

In 1904, Mr. C. K. Harley, of San Francisco, entered the game, with a string collected for him by Lyndon and containing about the pick of George Raper's kennels; but the Coast fancier after a few seasons dropped out. Major Carnochan, one of the old timers, has also been absent from the list of exhibitors for some years. Mr. Ingwersen of Chicago has long been a faithful supporter. There are always a scattering number of smaller owners all over the country, who support local shows and who once in a while make a dash at New York, but the bulk of the winnings are made by the Sabines and the Warrens. They have both turned out an amazing number of good home breds, and they have even sent a couple of their best over the ocean where they have been well able to hold their heads high even in the depth of English competition. Possibly the Sabines have the better of it in numbers of champions, but in my opinion, the one best smooth Fox Terrier that has been produced by American breeders is Warren Remedy, who at her best was about as near perfection as a dog man ever hopes to see.

One of the most encouraging things in Fox Terrierdom is the great number of very high qualified home breds that we see. Of course, the majority of these have come out of the big kennels, but what they can do can certainly be done by the smaller owners, for it is a well known fact that in most cases the greatest number of good home breds come from the more modest establishments. There is certainly enough good blood in the country to give our breeders the material with which to work. The opportunity is here, and the increasing number of Fox Terrier enthusiasts seems to indicate that that opportunity will not be wasted.

THE WIRE-HAIRED FOX TERRIER

CHAPTER III

THE WIRE-HAIRED FOX TERRIER

JUST because the smooth Fox Terrier had some fifteen or twenty years start in popular recognition over his wire coated brother, most people think that he is the original and that the wiry jacketed dog is but a mere sub-variety. This is a rank injustice—quite as unfair as it would to say that North Dakota is a sub-division of South Dakota, or *vice versa*—for each is an equally important variety of one and the same breed.

The usual theory is that the smooth is the older variety and that they, mated with various wire terriers common in the Border Counties of England a century ago, produced the wire-haired Fox Terrier. On the other hand, there are some careful students of terrier history who point out that the older terrier breeds of Great Britain were undoubtedly wire coated. On this fact, they base their claim that the shoe fits the other foot and that the smooth was probably developed from the wire by mating with the smooth coated Manchester Terrier.

As all Fox Terrier records—written, spoken, engraved, or painted—that antedate 1850 make but a scanty and fragmentary collection, there will probably never be any proof positive to settle this debate. If forced to register my guess (and this is all anyone can really do) I should be inclined to support the wire as the original product. This is not, I know, the usual belief, but as the wire terriers were in the majority at the time the breed was developed it seems the more probable explanation.

Guessing aside, we know that the smooth dog first "took on" and was pretty well known and generally appreciated when, in the late seventies, the wire dog made his bow at the bench shows. The English fanciers, accustomed to the smooth variety, hailed the "new" dogs as a freakish novelty. They, however, had in their looks, their intelligence, and their gameness the stuff of which a popular dog is made, and many friends were won to them. Now they are quite as popular and as well known as their smooth rivals. In America, however, they are not so generally known, except to the bench show cult—and even among

WIRE-HAIRED FOX TERRIER 41

those who know them there is more or less of the sub-division idea prevalent.

When the wire-haired Fox Terrier first went to the English shows, he was not honored with classes of his own; but competed in company with various other breeds under the elastic term of "Broken Coated Working Terriers." Here he sniffed noses with Irish, Welsh, Airedale, Dandie Dinmont and Bedlington Terriers and even sometimes met Yorkshires and Skyes. It was not until 1882 that they could be registered in the English Kennel Club Stud Book as "Wire-Haired Fox Terriers."

Tom Wootton of Nottingham was, we are told, very largely responsible for the introduction of the wire coated dog to the English dog fancy. He was seconded by Mr. Carrick and Mr. Shirley, the owners of two tap-root strains from which the dogs of to-day are descended. Venture was the dog that contributed to the former's early successes; while Mr. Shirley built upon the foundations laid by his dog Tip. Another notable dog of the early days was Thorn. Mated to a bitch called Tease, bred by Wootton, he got Workman. This dog was a giant in size, but he sired any number of good sons and daughters of normal size. He was the foundation of Mr. Harding Cox's famous Broad strain: his most signal success at stud being when mated to Kismet (by the smooth Ch. Old Turk) when two notable champions resulted, Mendicant Broad and Toiler Broad.

The Broom strain, owned by Mr. George Colmore, was still another important factor in the development of the breed. Mr. G. Welsh had a dog called Turk, who had the happy knack of getting the right sort of puppies. He was responsible for the sensational winner Ch. Miss Miggs. This celebrated bitch and Ch. Briggs were the backbone of Mr. Hayward Field's successful kennels, which he eventually sold for what was then a record price to Lord Lonsdale.

After this came Ch. Go Bang. He was bred by Mr. George Raper and after a long career full of bench honors he came to this country. Ch. Tipton Slasher was a winner at this time, and he was lucky enough to beat Go Bang at one of their meetings, but he is better known to-day as the sire of the dam of Ch. Cackler of Notts. Ch. Jack St. Leger, a very taking white dog, was a contemporary of those dogs who is worthy of mention.

Mr. Charles McNeill, with his Knavesmire Jest, founded the famous strain that is directly responsible for the very high quality of the wire hairs of yesterday and to-day. It is a

WIRE-HAIRED FOX TERRIER

strain that is famous throughout the world, and it has done wonders for the variety. Jest bred to Meersbrook Crissy got Ch. Meersbrook Bristles, the most important wire dog of all time. He was a great winner, sound, full of terrier character and with a jacket that lived up to his name. But it was in his head that he so greatly excelled. It was the first of those long, clean, aristocratic heads that we see to-day largely because Bristles put them on most of his puppies.

The main line of this most illustrious family comes down through Ch. Barkby Ben, grandson of Bristles. He in turn sired Ch. Cackler of Notts, whose son Ch. Commodore of Notts has lived up to his family's great reputation as breeders of winners. Master Bristles and Ch. Raby Matchbox, though not of this same branch, are other illustrious names in this family's records.

To-day, over in England, the wire-haired Fox Terrier is not only quite as popular as the smooth, but, as the usual thing, his quality is higher. Such dogs as Morden Bullseye, Southborough Salex, Roper's Nutcracker, Royston Remus, Coastguard, and Sylvan Result (all champions of yesterday) are names to conjure with in Fox Terrier circles and the smooths would have a hard time, despite all their great cracks, to find equally good contemporaries of these dogs.

In this country, it is a pretty even toss-up between the two varieties. We have certainly had more high qualitied home-bred smooths, but England has sent us over some very taking wires. In this matter of breeding, and I always have a soft spot in my heart for an American bred champion, the smooth fanciers have surely set a good example. With the general public, the smooth dog is better known and more popular, for unless one has a grounding in the essentials of terrier characteristics and requirements, he is apt to think the wire hair "odd looking." Among the fanciers, however, there are more showing wires than smooths. There is no one kennel as strong as either of the two biggest strings of smooths, but there are a goodly number of medium sized kennels scattered all over the country, and each season sees several new exhibitors competing for show honors.

The first show in America to give the wire-haired Fox Terrier a classification to himself was New York in 1883. Mr. Jack Grainger won with a dog called Tyke, who had been imported from Mr. Carrick's kennels, which have been mentioned as one of those that had an important bearing on the development of the breed in England. Tyke repeated this victory four years in succession, but competition was not very keen in those days. For several years the breed struggled along without making any marked impression. It did not catch the popular fancy quickly, but the growth, if slow, was healthy.

Mr. James Mortimer and Mr. Reginald H. Mayhew, both well known and popular judges, were among those who first supported the variety. Mr. H. H. Hunnewell, the secretary of the Fox Terrier Club, was another of the early American friends.

The New York Show of 1894 was the first at which the breed was given all of the usual classes divided according to sex, and by this time some real history was beginning to be made. Messrs. Hunnewell, Mortimer and Mayhew had been joined by other enthusiasts and there were plenty of entries and considerable quality. Mr. H. W. Smith and Mr. G. W. Ritchie both had very respectable entries in the classes: the former showing a very attractive pair in Cribbage and Janet. Mr. Hunnewell carried off top honors with his Oakleigh Bruiser, and Mr. Mayhew benched a real terrier in Brittle.

Shortly after this, one of our most important American kennels got its first celebrity and started on its successful career. This dog was Thornfield Knockout who was imported by Major Gouverneur M. Carnochan for his Cairnsmuir Kennels. Knockout proved to be a wise investment. He turned out to be a winner, and he was a marked success at stud, laying the foundations for this kennel. In his veins flowed the blood of the famous Meersbrook Bristles, and he came honestly by his ability to sire winners. Endcliff Banker was another early representative of this strain. Like Knockout he has gone down in history as the cornerstone of a good kennel, for to him is attributed the successful establishment of Mr. Lynn's kennels at Port Huron, Mich. His "one best get" was Bank Note, a big winner in his day.

That wire hair of all wire hairs, the great Ch. Meersbrook Bristles came to America in 1899. He was imported by Mr. C. W. Keys, of East Pepperell, Mass., and the opening of the twentieth century saw a number of nailing youngsters claiming him as sire. It is hard to over-estimate the importance of Bristles. As a show dog he was, in his prime, quite invincible, and his type is the one for which breeders to-day strive. What is rather remarkable, he was as great a sire as he was a bench winner. Other dogs in other breeds have had possibly

WIRE-HAIRED FOX TERRIER 47

more successful show careers: other dogs have "set the style" in their own variety; other dogs have made great names as sires of champions—but no other terrier of any breed has combined these three things to anywhere near the degree that did Meersbrook Bristles. We have already seen how the leading English strains trace directly back to him, and American fanciers can only regret that we did not have more good bitches to send to him and that he did not spend more of his days in our midst.

Before the importation of Bristles, Major Carnochan had brought over that sterling show dog, Ch. Go Bang, one of the best wires of all time. He was not, however, so useful in the breeding kennels as in the show ring, though his owner got from him that exceptionally successful home-bred Ch. Cairnsmuir Growler. Ch. Barkby Ben, of the main line of the Bristles' strain, followed Go Bang to Cairnsmuir. Like his famous grandsire, this dog was a combination show dog and sire. He was the last important dog brought over by Major Carnochan, who has not been exhibiting of late years. His last showing was done with a home-bred called, unless I am mistaken, Cairnsmuir Outlaw.

Hope springs eternal, and it is some consolation to know that the kennels at New City, N. Y., are never completely empty, and it does seem that there is always at least a fighting chance that the Cairnsmuirs may someday be with us again.

Just about the time that Major Carnochan was withdrawing from the field, three kennels, which if short lived, were at their time very important, were having their short innings. Mr. Knowles, of Magnolia, Mass.; Mr. Harley, of San Francisco; and Mr. McComb, of New York City, each in succession took up the wire-coated Fox Terrier and started in seriously to collect the right sort of materials for successful kennels. It was most unfortunate that each in turn was forced to retire just at the time that they were beginning to make some real headway. Mr. Harley had a very taking sort of terrier in his Ch. Wandee Coastguard, and Mr. Scott McComb had quite a collection of cracks, especially in bitches, his best being the great Ch. Dusky Siren, who when at her best, was about as nice a wire hair as has been seen.

The places left empty by the breaking up of these kennels have been filled not by three big kennels, but by a score of more modest ones. Philadelphia has quite a coterie of fanciers headed by Mr. Robert Strawbridge and Boston is a veritable hotbed of "wire fanciers." There is usually a strong contender or two hailing from Down East. New York is hardly so strong, but the interest in the breed is growing. Mr. Daniel S. Riker, of Airedale fame, is a recent convert of the right sort in the metropolitan district. Chicago Airedale circles have also been drafted for wire Fox Terrier recruits, and the Niolas have been joined by the Vickery Kennels and more lately by Mr. Francis Porter. Throughout the middle west there are quite a number of smaller kennels that can be depended upon to make things interesting and to see to it that all the blues do not go home with one kennel.

Both varieties of the Fox Terrier are coming strong, and which will eventually become the more popular with American fanciers is a matter of preference for a smooth or a wire jacket. Both have sound constitutions, good tempers, intelligence, and gameness. Both are deservingly popular in England and many fanciers over there go in both varieties. Either one is hard to beat for a trappy, sporty dog, good to look at and desirable as a pal.

THE TERRIER'S EDUCATION

CHAPTER IV

THE TERRIER'S EDUCATION

TRAINING, education, and specialization are all familiar terms these days. It is acknowledged that the skilled dwarf is more powerful than the ignorant giant; that the efficiency of the genius is increased many times by proper schooling. So it is with dogs. By nature and by the art of breeding these terriers have been endowed with gifts fitting them to do whatever a good dog may be called upon to do, but proper training will enable them to do it more easily and better.

With a dog of so many talents it is somewhat difficult to decide just the best way in which to take up the different branches of his education, but let us divide the training upon the basis of a terrier in town and in the country.

Dogs will always be kept in the cities as companions, and I suppose that it is useless to say that a Harlem flat is just about the worst place in the world for a dog. Any terrier just cries for room. He is lively as a cricket and as full of spirits as a nut is of kernel—both excellent qualities in any dog outside a flat. The city at best is no place for any dog; no place for terriers of all dogs. Yet hundreds of dogs live in town and they serve their purpose. Also, they have a great deal to learn.

House-breaking

House-breaking is the first lesson that has to be taught the city dog. Usually it saves time and money to see that the dog you buy is already so trained, but this cannot always be done. It is a risky business to guarantee a dog house-broken, and too much faith must not be placed in any such promises. It often happens that, while a dog will always behave perfectly in one house, he may have to be trained all over again when introduced into another. This is mainly true of puppies, so you need not consider yourself basely deceived if, in this particular, a youngster does not live strictly up to the recommendations of his seller.

If your dog arrives in a crate, he should, the very first thing after unpacking, be given a run. The safest way to bring him into the house is on a lead and to keep him tied up short in some convenient place for a couple of days, taking him out regularly at fixed hours. He will soon get into these habits. Should he offend, he ought to be punished at the scene of his crime, taking care that he is aware of his offense, and tied up again. A very few days of this treatment will house-break any dog who is old enough to understand what you are driving at. Trying to house-break a very young puppy is cruelty pure and simple.

Punishing a Dog

In punishing a dog, do not beat him about the ears and never use either a fine whip, or a stick. It has happened twice in my knowledge that a dog has had his hearing seriously damaged by a rupturing of the ear drums caused by blows on the head. A whip will cut the skin of a dog and a stick may break a bone. A smart slap under the jaw, accompanied by a word-scolding in a severe tone and uncompromising manner, is a thousand times better. In extreme cases, a strap may be used, but always remember that the object is not to flog the dog into cowardly and broken submission, but merely to impress upon him that he is not doing as you wish.

In all cases, it is best to punish a dog " red handed," but in no case should you punish him "red headed." Unless the dog knows for what he is being punished, you are like Xerxes whipping the Hellespont for wrecking his ships, except that a dog has more feelings than the sea. The best way to be sure that the dog knows is to catch him in the very act. This has the disadvantage, however, of making it likely that you will be in a temper.

No dog should ever be punished when you have not perfect control over yourself. The patience of Job was never tried by a healthy terrier puppy, or it might have reached its limits. A spoiled rug, the flower-beds wrecked, a new hat chewed up, slippers and rubbers all over the house, religious disobedience, all these things do cultivate a temper, but temper and dog-training do not live together successfully.

In training a dog, be sure that he knows exactly what you want him to do, and then be sure that he always does it. Make obedience a habit. In time, it will come as natural to him as breathing. When you say, "Come here," see that he comes, and let him understand that "Lie down" means just that and nothing more. It is very useful to have a dog that lives in the house "stay-put" when placed in a chair or a corner, and this should be part of his education. It is very bad dog-manners to jump on visitors. Even to those who love dogs it is often disagreeable.

Personally I am not in favor of teaching a dog tricks. A trick dog soon learns to "love the limelight," and will be continually begging to be allowed to show off. Besides, I have an inborn dislike to seeing a dog "doing stunts," and I know the feeling is shared by others who are fond of a good dog. It seems a silly thing to see a big, strong terrier begging, or walking on his hind legs. It may be very clever for poodles and pugs, but with a man's dog—and the terriers are all "man's dogs"—it always calls to my mind a painting in the Louvre in which Hercules is depicted sitting at the feet of Venus industriously winding up a ball of yarn. However, tastes differ, and these tricks are all easy to teach a bright pupil who has already learned the lesson of minding.

When the city dog goes out for a walk, his training gets its real test. What a lovely spectacle it is to see a dog owner rushing and yelling after a dog who runs about, paying no more attention to his master than to the clouds overhead. It is a sight that has but one equal, that of a portly, pompous gentleman chasing his own hat.

Even if a dog is perfectly trained indoors, he may break loose when first taken out on the street. He can, however, easily be made to understand that his master is to be boss on the street, as well as in the house. One of the best habits a city dog can have is that of keeping close to his owner's heels crossing streets. A dog is perfectly well able to cross a crowded street, but in busy thoroughfares a dog and his master are apt to get separated, and all may not be so fortunate as the Washington physician who had his champion Airedale returned with a note which read:

"Dear Doc—Here is your Yeller Dog. Will you Plese give me 15 cents i hate to ask so much but i had to fead him 2 days."

Country Training

The terrier who lives in the country is more fortunate than his brother in town. His preliminary education is just the same, but he gets a college course in hunting, and maybe a little post-graduate work in cattle driving. All that has been said about house-breaking and teaching to mind applies with equal force to the country dog. If there are not so many interested spectators to make it embarrassing, it is just as provoking to have a runaway dog in the meadows and pastures as in the streets and avenues. A single motor at sixty or seventy

THE TERRIER'S EDUCATION 59

miles an hour on the turnpike is harder for a dog to dodge than the whole flood of traffic that streams up and down the city thoroughfares. So, city or country, teach your dog to mind.

Any terrier will take as naturally to rats, woodchucks, and such vermin as a lot of little yellow ducklings will to the mill pond. But to make assurance doubly sure, it is best to introduce him to mice, or small rats, when he is four or five months old. This is the way terriers are broken in England. It has been found that if a terrier is jumped bang at Mr. Woodchuck, for example, he may be spoiled by biting off the first time more than he can chew.

The gradual system of breaking applied to water is best. Practically all terriers will swim naturally without any training at all, but once in a while there comes along one who does not take to water. He should be coaxed in, not taken by the scruff of the neck and pitched overboard. Methods like that, when dogs are concerned, are not generally successful.

In driving cattle and sheep the terrier is going into a new trade, as it were, and not one to which he was born. He proves his versatility by the quickness with which he can learn to be an excellent drover. The easiest way is to take him out with a dog experienced in this work. If this cannot be done, one will have to train him himself, and this is not so difficult as it sounds, but it is best to make sure that the dog has carefully learned that minding trick above mentioned before undertaking this.

All dogs are naturally watch-dogs, but terriers, because of their size and intelligence, are particularly good ones. It is not the wisest policy to chain up a dog at night, for he will be much more apt to sound false alarms, and in any case of real need he is powerless to give active defense of himself or his friends. The watch-dog ought not to have his big meal at night, or he will go to sleep and snore peacefully till cock crow. If fed but lightly, he will rest in a series of cat naps,—if a dog can do that.

TERRIERS IN HEALTH

CHAPTER V

TERRIERS IN HEALTH

ONE of the most noted veterinarians in New York once said to me that, if it were not for too much or too little attention, he doubted if he should ever be called upon to treat a dog. He explained his meaning by adding that the toy dogs are generally killed by kindness and most terriers die of neglect. If this is true, and this doctor has a canine practice that keeps him busy from morning till night, there must be something radically wrong with the care of most dogs.

The terriers—for the evils of a candy diet and a life spent on silken pillows do not need to be even mentioned here—the terriers can, it is perfectly true, get along with less attention than most breeds of dogs, for they all have wonderful constitutions. Does that, however, give the terrier owner a free right and license to neglect his dogs?

Essentials for Health

It is almost a joke to keep such a naturally healthy dog as a terrier in the pink of condition. All he needs is dry, clean kennels, with decent bedding; good, nourishing food at regular hours; all the fresh water he wants to drink; plenty of exercise, and a little grooming. Given these few things and a terrier will be " disgustingly well," full of high spirits, and happy as a clam at high tide. It is really so easy to keep a terrier " fit," and it means so much to the dog and his owner, whether he be a dog owner for pleasure or for profit, that it is nothing less than criminal not to do so.

Kennels, bedding, food and feeding, water, exercise, and grooming—these are the things which given proper attention mean a healthy and happy dog. Let us take them up, one at a time, for it is as often ignorance as thoughtlessness that causes the trouble.

Kennels

The question as to the kind of a kennel is bound to have a variety of different answers, according to whether one lives in the city or the country, in the North or the South, and whether one is to keep one dog or fifty.

There are, however, certain fundamental considerations that apply to any home for dogs.

In the first place, all terriers, especially those wearing those wonderful, double, weather-proof garments we call "wire coats," are healthier living the simple life out of doors. This is true in any climate. I used to have all sorts of troubles with the skins and coats of my wire terriers till I just turned them out, providing them with dry, draft-proof, but unheated shelters in which to sleep and where they could escape very bad weather.

My own experience has proved to me that wire coated terriers are worlds better off for being out every day and night in the year. Even in the severest weather they do not need artificial heat, if they have a perfectly dry, draftless, well bedded place to sleep in and to serve as a shelter on wet, stormy days. A decent kennel for any dog from a St. Bernard to a Pomeranian is dry and draft-proof, and the terrier owner can therefore eliminate the question of artificial heating.

The man who lives in the city should try to keep his dog out in the yard as much as possible, and, if at all feasible, let him sleep there. Dogs have an inborn instinct to "bay the moon" and terriers are supposed to be great talkers. Moreover, city backyards, since the days when town residences were hollow stone piles lined with hides to keep the wind out, have always been a favorite *rendezvous* for Thomas Catt, Esq., and Mistress Tabby, meetings just as hard on the nerves of a self respecting terrier as they are on those of his sleepy master. The trouble is that, while master becomes a public benefactor by hurling his shaving mug out the window, the efforts of his dog to drive away the disturbers are regarded by the unsympathetic neighbors as quite as bad as the feline serenades and battle cries. No dog will bark at night if he is in a dark, quiet place, and the terrier in the backyard will sleep like a baby, providing he is shut up in a box covered with burlap or old sacking.

The ideal terrier kennel is an oil barrel. These cannot always be obtained, but any barrel or keg intended to hold liquids, and so made water tight, will answer. A hole, just large enough to let the dog in and out, should be cut in one end. Then the inside may be painted with kerosene and a lighted paper dropped in. This cleans the barrel and destroys any insects, and is an excellent thing to do every month or so.

The barrel ought to be painted inside and out, and to keep it from rotting on the bottom must be mounted on blocks so that it just clears the ground. Rain can be kept out of the door either by tacking a curtain of sacking over it (a dog soon learns to go through this and it can be hung up in good weather) or by making a V-shaped roof of planking, which sets over the barrel, projecting in front like the eaves of a barn. Two small terriers can live easily in these keg-kennels in summer, with an extra dog added, for warmth's sake, in cold weather.

Another kennel which is fine for terriers is one I adapted from the suggestions of a chicken owner, who used a similar box as a coop for hens with young chicks. It is a box that can be taken all apart. The floor is a raised platform against which the sides fit closely, being fastened together with hooks. The roof slants backward and is held in place by thin strips that fit just inside the walls.

This is excellent for summer, but must be very carefully made to be tight enough for cold weather. Having a flat floor, it is admirable for a bitch with puppies and it has the additional advantage of enabling you to leave off one side in hot weather. Naturally, they are very easy to clean. Your carpenter can make them any size or shape you wish, costing from five dollars up.

For the man who is going into a large kennel, little can be said that will be broadly useful.

One wants to build a model kennel of hard wood and concrete, while the next has an old chickenhouse to adapt to doggy uses; naturally requirements and conditions are very different.

The first thing that any kennel builder wants is good natural drainage and runs that are on quickly drying ground, gravel rather than clay. Southern exposures are the favorite, and it is better to have two or three smaller buildings, rather than to house all the dogs in one. In this way there is opportunity to give each building a rest once in a while, and this should be done in the case of the individual runs and pens, if not for the whole building.

Good hard wood, varnished and kept clean, and well drained, is the most popular floor for kennels. Concrete is cold in winter, asphalt is far from desirable in summer, and both are hard on a dog's feet. Dirt, gravel, and ashes are very hard to clean. Cork is expensive and rots out with amazing speed.

The sleeping benches ought to be about two feet off the floor and so arranged that they can be taken down, cleaned, and set out in the sun to dry. Plenty of elbow grease, backed up with a good strong disinfectant and fresh air and sunlight: these are the secrets of a successful kennel. Cleanliness means that disease and parasites will be unknown.

Wheat or rye straw, or wood shavings make the best bedding. The straw costs more than hay, but it is ten times as cleanly, lasts twice as long, and is much better for a dog's skin. Very often shavings will be given away for the carting of them, and they make a fine summer bedding, though they are not very warm for winter. Shavings, especially pine shavings, make a poor home for fleas. Excelsior is not popular. It has a distressing habit of wadding up in hard bunches in corners, absorbs moisture, and does not dry out easily. Moss, sea weed, and such beddings are dirty and hard to handle.

Food

Food is an important item in the care of the dog. Table scraps make, in my opinion, the ideal food. In this the house pet has the advantage over his friend of the kennels, for he gets a wide variety of well cooked and nourishing food; and variety, cooking, and nourishment are the whole story of good feeding.

Dog biscuits, which are so cheap and easy to handle, are excellent in their way, but one should resist the temptation to feed them all the time. You would not like to live on beefsteak three times a day, week in and week out,

Dry bread can be bought by the barrel from most bakers and is at once inexpensive and nourishing. Shredded wheat scraps and broken crackers can also be purchased and are useful for a change. All of these should be fed soaked in some soup.

In the winter, I have found corn meal very acceptable, but the moment hot weather comes along its use should be discontinued, or skin troubles will surely result. It can either be made in a mush with milk or water, or baked into corn bread cakes.

I use a homemade dog biscuit from corn meal and meat made at home in the following way. The meat stock is boiled over night in a kettle and the unstrained soup is used with the meal in making dough. This is put in pans two or three inches deep and baked till hard all the way through in a slow oven. The baking will take a day. These cakes are rich and should not be fed too often, but they can be kept a month, and I never saw a terrier that did not relish them. In summer, fish boiled twenty-four hours, till the bones are all soft, makes a nice change from the meat soups of the winter.

There are many who might be called canine vegetarians, but experimenting has convinced me that meat is the best and most natural food for the dog. Sirloin does cost a lot of money these days, but hearts, lungs, heads, odds and ends of ribs, and shank bones are not expensive, and you can always make arrangements with a butcher to save you these. Under no circumstances feed meat that is decayed. It does not have to be as fresh as you demand for your own table, if you take care to cook it thoroughly, but meat that is mouldy or rotting is poison, not food.

Most kennels feed twice a day,—a light lunch in the morning and the regular day's meal in the evening. The morning bite can be bread or biscuits with a little soup over them. The evening meal ought to be all that the dog will comfortably eat without stuffing. If any food is left in the dishes, it should be cleaned away before night; and the dog who is "off his feed" should have attention.

Dogs vary as much as people in the amount they will eat. One gobbler may be always thin, while a dainty eater may put on more flesh than necessary. It is the height of foolishness to pamper a dog's taste and make him an epicure, but neither is it wise to treat them all just alike.

Exercise

Exercise naturally follows feeding in our consideration of the health of the dog. Exercise, and plenty of it, is the best tonic. It keeps the muscles hard and the stomach in shape; it prevents fatness, and is just play for a dog.

There is, however, exercise and exercise. To walk a dog along on a lead is exercise, but three minutes' free running is worth half an hour of "taking the dog out for a walk" after the manner of the young lady who lives in the city. Each kennel should have an exercising yard, a lot as big as possible, where the dogs can be turned out for a romp. One should be a little careful about leaving a lot of dogs turned out together, for their likes and dislikes are as strong as our own.

I remember with sorrow an experience of this kind. A recently purchased dog was added to a run full of home bred youngsters, and because he was older and bigger he played the bully till one bright morning three of his victims combined forces and gave him a lesson in manners. It was also a lesson for his owner. The dog's ear was so chewed that he was ruined for showing.

Grooming

The last item in the care of the dog is grooming, but it is at least as important as any of the others we have taken up. Most dogs are washed too often and not brushed often enough. Washing once in two weeks in summer and once a month in winter is all that is needed to keep a terrier clean, but he should be brushed daily.

In washing a dog, start at the head with a good disinfecting soap and work backwards and downwards, for fleas make for the head when threatened with drowning, and only in this way can these pests be gotten rid of. It is well to let the soap stay in the coat a few minutes, but it must be all washed out very carefully before drying the dog.

The daily grooming should consist first of a combing with a fairly fine comb, to clean out matted dirt and hair. This should be followed by a sharp brushing with what is called in the stable a dandy brush. The finishing touches must be a rub down with a hound glove, such as is sold in the kennel supply stores. This treatment will keep a terrier in almost perfect show form all the time, and the stimulation of the skin will be found to act as a regular tonic.

Housed in clean, draftless kennels; given good food with lots of exercise, and with some little attention bestowed on his toilet, a terrier is sure to be healthy and happy. Prevention is proverbially better than cure, and the little work of keeping a terrier well is nothing compared to the care of a sick dog. Dogs do not make very pleasant patients, and there is the added difficulty in finding out just what really ails them, for even the most intelligent of our animals cannot tell us where his aches are and how a dose of certain medicine affects him.

DISEASES AND REMEDIES

CHAPTER VI

DISEASES AND REMEDIES

THE terrier owner is a "lucky devil," for his dogs do not, as a rule, spend a great deal of time in the hospital. All members of the terrier family, from the giant of the race, the Airedale, way down to little Scottie, owe a big debt to Nature for having blessed them with remarkably robust constitutions. They do not catch cold from every draft. They throw off the various contagious diseases. Even when really sick, they make wonderfully rapid recoveries.

All dog flesh, however, is heir to certain diseases, and even the most healthy and strong are not exceptions to this rule. Many of the books on doggy subjects are so deep and technical that the poor novice, who has waded through their sonorous and involved phrases, is really more at sea about how to treat his sick dog than before he took them from the shelf. Other books on dogs, especially the popular ones, are so brief in their descriptions that no amount of study of them can teach much. It is my object to steer between these two extremes and to tell something of the common ailments, so that everyone may understand their causes, recognize their symptoms, and prescribe various treatments.

Two good rules for the amateur veterinarian to learn at the very outset are: In case of any doubt, or if the trouble is at all serious, time, money, and maybe the dog's life will be saved by calling at once upon a registered D. V. S.; secondly, a dog's ailments are nine times out of ten the same, with the same symptoms and results, as in ourselves. A dog, therefore, can receive the same treatment as people, for the medicines act upon him just as upon yourself. In the case of the terriers, the dose is one-fourth of that for an adult human. To use more commonsense than medicine is another good rule, for nursing and a little attention to diet often effect a cure without any drugs at all.

Remembering that the same treatment that you would give yourself cures your dogs makes it unnecessary to go into such ailments as cuts, burns, colds, stomach disorders, and poisons. There are, however, some distinctively canine ailments. For convenience, let us take these up alphabetically.

Canker of the Ear

Canker of the ear is not by any means so common in terriers as in the long-eared breeds, but it sometimes affects dogs who go a great deal in the water, though it may be caused by some foreign substance getting into the ear. There are two forms—the external and the internal. The external shows itself by sores on ear flaps, which are most painful and cause the dog to scratch and paw at his ear. The sores ought to be cleaned thoroughly with hot water and dressed with zinc ointment daily. In bad cases, the head may be bandaged to prevent aggravation of the ulcers by scratching.

The internal form is harder to cure. Its symptoms are hot, inflamed ears, pain, pawing, and rubbing the head against the floor or walls. The interior of the ear should be douched out with warm water and boracic acid or witch hazel, and then syringed with a solution of one part of spirits of wine and twenty parts of water. Afterwards the ear should be carefully dried out with cotton on the end of a pencil—care must be taken not to injure the interior of the ear—and finally dusted with boracic acid. The treatment should be given every evening and morning till all signs of the trouble have disappeared.

CHOREA

Chorea, or, as it is sometimes called, St. Vitus's Dance, is generally a legacy of distemper. It is a peculiar nervous twitching, generally affecting the forelegs and shoulders. It is almost incurable, but good food, exercise, and a tonic may work wonders.

CRAMPS

Cramps in the hindquarters may sometimes attack a dog who goes a great deal into the water and they are not unknown as a result of cold and damp kennels, or great exposure to cold. The symptoms are a more or less complete paralysis of the hind legs, accompanied by great pain. The dog should be given a hot bath and the affected parts, after a careful drying, should be rubbed well with chloroform liniment.

DIARRHOEA

Diarrhoea, which may be caused by food or worms, can usually be stopped by a mild purge of half castor oil and half syrup of buckthorn, which may be followed by a dose of prepared chalk. Boiled rice is an excellent food for dogs suffering from disordered bowels. Any disturbance of this nature is more a symptom than a disease and the cause must be removed before a cure can be made.

Distemper

Distemper is the bane of the dog owner's existence. It is a highly contagious disease generally attacking puppies, and is comparable to scarlet fever in that one attack successfully gone through usually means immunity. It was formerly thought that distemper could arise spontaneously from improper feeding or unsanitary kenneling, but the germ of the disease has been isolated, and while poor food and dirty kennels increase the chances of the disease by lowering the dog's resistance, they are not in themselves causes.

The distemper germ is possessed of remarkable vitality and may be transferred either directly from dog to dog or through the medium of crates, bedding, clothing, and even the air. Shows are a source of spreading the disease, though there is much less danger of this now than formerly, for the veterinary inspection and proper disinfecting methods have improved conditions wonderfully. A bitch from an infected kennel may give distemper to the inmates of the kennels she visits for breeding purposes. Plenty of soap and water, disinfectant, and elbow grease make a distemper preventive that is much better than any cure.

The discovery of the distemper germ has naturally resulted in the making of an antitoxin, by attenuating the virus till a weakened form is obtained. Using this to inoculate a well dog, a mild form of the disease attacks him, but this " vaccination " has not proved unqualifiedly successful, especially when used by amateurs.

The commonest form of distemper is catarrhal, with symptoms much like those of an ordinary cold, lack of appetite, fever, disordered bowels, vomiting, staring coat, rapid loss of flesh, and discharges from the nose and eyes. The distemper germ, however, may attack other organs than the nose and eyes. The lungs and bronchial tubes and the stomach and intestines are also seats of the trouble. These forms are harder to diagnose and harder to cure. The presence of dysentery and sometimes of jaundice are indications that the digestive tract is involved.

I know of no sure cure for distemper, and I never knew of a dog owner who did, though, to be sure, they all have their favorite remedies. There are no end of patent specifics on the market, and some of these are very good, but the best thing for a tyro to do is to call a veterinarian. Leave the doctoring to him, at least till you have had the experience gained by a couple of good cases of distemper in your kennels. There will be plenty for you to do without bothering about prescribing.

The dog with distemper must be isolated, and you must take the precautions that you would if there were smallpox in the neighborhood. Wash with disinfectants, burn sulphur candles, scrupulously destroy all bedding—use all the knowledge of antiseptic disinfecting that you have.

As for the patient, you will find that nursing is just as important as medicine—in fact, the more I have to do with the disease, the less medicine I administer and the more care I give to nursing. Keep up the dog's strength with almost any sick room food that he will eat. Raw meat, eggs, gruels, soups, milk, all these are good, and the dog should be fed often. The discharges from the nose and eyes should be wiped away regularly.

If the nose becomes very badly stopped up, so that breathing is difficult, the dog's head may be held over a pail of hot water in which a little turpentine has been dropped and made to inhale the fumes. If the throat and bronchial tubes are affected, give a little cough syrup—any one will do, but be careful not to give enough to upset the stomach. See that the dog has plenty of water to drink and keep him out of all drafts, though the room must be well ventilated for fresh air is good medicine in these cases.

Fits

Fits seem to be a part of the life of most puppies. They are not dangerous and usually pass off without bad effects. But fits are a symptom, and the cause should be removed. They may be caused by worms, stomach troubles, or heat. Keep the dog quiet and give him a dose of castor oil and buckthorn, but find the cause and remove it.

Insects

Insects of several kinds take pleasure in seeing to it that neither the dog or his owner gets lazy. The commonest and the easiest to get rid of are fleas, but they are dangerous as being the cause of tapeworm, for the tapeworm of the dog spends part of his life (in the larva form) in the fleas. There are any number of good flea soaps on the market and a dozen good flea powders, so little need be said about ridding the dog of these pests.

Lice are harder to get rid of, but the dog can be freed of them in the same way as of fleas. Care should be taken to get rid of as many as possible of the lice eggs, little black specks that stick to the hair.

Ticks are the least common, but because of their habit of burrowing into the skin cannot be washed out. The best way is to give the dog a good rubbing in a dressing composed of olive and kerosene oils, equal parts of each, followed by a bath.

Kennel Lameness

Kennel lameness, or rheumatism, affects a dog similarly to human beings, there being a soreness of certain parts—usually the fore-shoulders or back—and pain, sometimes with swelling of the joints. The dog should be kept in a light, dry, well-ventilated place, his bowels kept open, and the food given, light but nourishing. A little sodium bicarbonate or sodium salicylate added to his drinking water will be found to be beneficial, and hot baths and rubbings with liniments ease the pain considerably.

Skin Diseases

Skin diseases are among the common troubles of the dog owner, for there are three varieties. The wire terriers seem to suffer a good deal from eczema—this is especially true of Scotties—and their owner is sure to know it before he has been in the game very long. It is a skin disease, noncontagious, arising from the blood and showing itself in red eruptions which burst, oozing their contents and forming scabs. Their hair comes off, and by scratching the dog aggravates the condition.

High feeding and too little exercise are the usual cause of the trouble, and the root of the matter must be reached before a cure can be effected. A good purge should be given, and the dog put on a light, simple diet. The sores should be washed clean and then treated with a wash of four parts of sugar of lead and one part of zinc sulphate in water. Fowler's Solution is also given sometimes, but this is a poison and ought not to be administered save on a veterinarian's advice.

There are two forms of mange—sarcoptic and follicular—both highly infectious, and the latter so hard to cure that many dog owners would almost rather kill a dog than go through the siege, with the constant danger of inoculating other dogs. The sarcoptic form is more on the surface and attacks dogs under the legs, which become red and inflamed, little reddish pimples forming, which break and form dark red scabs. The follicular mange usually starts on the back near the tail or over the collar. The hair falls out, red scabs form and there is a peculiar odor. It is difficult to tell just which form one is dealing with after the case has gone far, but at the outset it is comparatively easy.

Both of these manges are caused by parasites which live in the skin. The microscope reveals them, and this is the only way that one, at the outset, can be perfectly sure he is dealing with mange and not eczema. The dog should be thoroughly cleaned and then dressed with the following ointment: creosote ½ oz.; oil of cade 1 oz.; zinc ointment and lanoline each 3 ozs.; and sulphur ½ oz. This is not a pretty or a nice mixture, but it has done the work more than once for me. The main thing with mange is cleanliness and keeping everlastingly at it. Skipping a day in the treatment will add a week to the cure. Sarcoptic mange caught in time can be cured in two weeks. Follicular mange may take three months, or even longer, to be cured completely.

Worms

Worms are almost sure to be found in all dogs not regularly treated for them, and they are the cause of a good deal of trouble. Puppies are favorite victims for these internal parasites, and youngsters who serve as hosts for these undesirable visitors never do well. Worms come from fleas, sheep and cattle stomachs and intestines, and sheep heads. Three varieties are common—the round, thread, and the tape, the last being the most dangerous.

Puppies should be given a good vermifuge when weaned, and the treatment should be kept up all through the dog's life. Emaciation, vomiting, bloating of the stomach, bad breath, and dragging the rectum along the ground after stool are the usual evidences of worms, but the wise dog owner does not wait for such signs. There are several good, prepared vermifuges on the market, usually containing santonin, male fern, or acerca nut, but naturally I do not feel that this is the place to mention them by name. Almost any of them will do the work if the manufacturer's directions are followed.

Administering Medicines

In conclusion, a word or two about giving

DISEASES AND REMEDIES

medicines may be useful. The best way to hold a terrier is to sit in a low chair and place him so that his body is under you and his shoulders between your knees. To give a pill you do not need help for so small a dog. By putting your left hand over his mouth and pressing you can force him to open his mouth by forcing his lips against his teeth. Lift up his head and put the pill as far back as you can on his tongue and hold his mouth closed till he has swallowed.

With liquids you will need an assistant to pour the medicine into the natural funnel you make of the dog's mouth by pulling his lips on one side out. In this, you do not open the mouth, but merely hold up the head. The medicine should be poured slowly between the teeth and lips, and the mouth held closed till the dose is swallowed.

Let me again impress the importance of remembering the similarity of canine and human ills. It is also well to bear in mind that careful nursing is usually very much better than dosing. This is especially true when the dosing is done by one who is not perfectly sure just what he is doing and why he is doing it.

THE SCIENCE OF DOG BREEDING

CHAPTER VII

THE SCIENCE OF DOG BREEDING

THE principles upon which Darwin based his theory of evolution—which are now accepted by scientists the world over as biological laws—are the very same as those under which the dog breeder works. Modern animal breeding is evolution in which man plays Dame Nature's part.

Breeding is, however, far from being an exact science, though it is continually becoming more and more scientific in its methods. We cannot sit down, a pencil in our fingers and paper before us, and with the aid of the Stud Book and a set of mathematical formulas, figure out a dog that will surely be a champion. We can, however, by supplementing the scientific data biologists have collected in their research work with the lore and traditions of the kennels, come nearer and nearer to the breeder's ideal of "a champion in every litter."

It is quite obvious that working with such plastic materials, we can never hope to have a perfectly uniform product, but who would have it so? Dog breeding is now more uncertain than roulette, twice as fascinating as the stock market, as interesting as auction bridge. Make it a matter of mathematically exact rules, working out as invariably and regularly as a machine, and the charm has vanished.

The three principles of Darwin's theory of how and why evolution acts are heredity, variation and selection. The law of heredity says that like will produce like; two bull terriers will have bull terriers. The law of variation says that no two dogs, even if they be of the same litter, will ever be exactly alike even in the smallest details. No two St. Bernards were ever alike, nor were the smallest teeth of the two smallest Pomeranians ever identical. There is ample evidence to show that the chemical composition of the muscles, bones, and blood of two animals of the same species are different, and from time to time vary considerably in one individual. The law of selection is the law of the struggle for existence, the survival of the fittest. The three laws together make up the theory of evolution by means of natural selection.

SCIENCE OF DOG BREEDING

Artificial Selection

What man does in breeding is the making and improving of species by artificial selection. He takes advantage of the law of heredity to establish breeds. If, however, like always exactly reproduced like, that is as far as he could ever get, but because there is infinite variation, the offspring differ from their parents. By selecting those that come nearest his ideal, the breeder does just what Dame Nature does when she kills off the physically unfit.

Since earliest times, man, more or less without thought or any knowledge of the whys and wherefores, has been carrying on scientific breeding in an unscientific way. Ever since he has kept domestic animals, his selection, formerly more or less unconscious, has been exerting its powerful force. For generations, the dog fanciers have been doing this; picking out the dogs and bitches most to their liking and mating them. The result is that although breeds of dogs are closely enough related to interbreed, some are of comparative age, and all breed wonderfully true to type.

Until quite recently, the dog breeders have been following the old, unscientific method, with some additional effort to correct faulty points in their dogs. That is, they have picked out individuals for breeding stock as near as possible to their ideals, and if the prospective mother was bad in head, they selected a stud dog strong in this point; while a very good coated matron might be mated to a poor coated dog provided he possessed marked excellencies in other directions.

Unfortunately but very scant attention was paid to the dams. This was largely from economical considerations, which led them to believe—or think they did merely because they wanted to—that " any old bitch with a pedigree was good enough to breed from." To bolster up their economy, they said that the pups inherited their looks from their sire and their dispositions from their dam.

Line Breeding

Two changes have taken place in the past decade. Breeders now know that physically, as well as mentally, the dam is quite as important as the sire. Moreover, they have learned that individual characteristics, however marked they may appear to be, do not have the force of family traits. In other words, a short, thick headed bitch bred to the longest headed dog alive would have short headed pups, if that dog had short headed parents and grandparents. These two fundamental bits of

SCIENCE OF DOG BREEDING

knowledge, learned originally from the biologists, have had a big effect on breeding operations.

A logical outgrowth of the importance that has been placed on family, with the naturally lessened emphasis on the individual, has been an increased number of the devotees of " line," rather than " in-breeding." In-breeding is beyond all doubt the strongest weapon the dog breeder has, but it is a boomerang that is very apt to come back and knock its thrower in the head. In-breeding is the breeding together of the blood of one dog—mother to son, or brother to sister. Line-breeding is the mating of dogs of the same general family, comparable to second or third cousins among human beings.

These breeding experiments fix the good and bad points of a dog, or a strain, very strongly. Carried to an extreme, they result in bad constitutions, lack of gameness, and, in extreme cases, in actual deformity. Such breeding demands that only the strongest and youngest dogs be mated.

Commonsense Breeding Rules

In selecting a sire, one should pick out a dog of recognized breeding, whose ancestors were dogs of the type you desire. A winner and a son of winners has better chances of being a sire of winners than an unknown dog of doubtful family. It is not wise, however, to rush to the latest champion. A popular bench hero is apt to be over-worked at stud. If your bitch is very young, send her to an older dog, and vice versa. Best results are not obtained if the dogs are over eight years old—that is a very good age limit at which to retire them from active service.

Most people know that a bitch comes in season, or is "in heat," fairly regularly at six months' intervals, and that this is the only time she will have sexual connection with a dog. The terriers generally come into their first heat when eight or nine months old and are remarkable for the regularity of their periods. The first sign is a swelling of the external parts and bleeding. After a week or ten days the bleeding is followed by a thickish, white discharge. This is the time to breed her. A bitch may be bred at her first heat, if she is not too young and is strong and healthy.

One service is all that is necessary—the old-timers to the contrary notwithstanding. Two services were formerly given, but this is no longer done by the best breeders. The time of gestation is only sixty-three days, and the second service, two days after the first, has been suspected of destroying the effect of the former. Statistics show that there are fewer misses and just as many puppies when there is but one service, as when there are two. The single service is obviously a great saving of the energies of the stud dog, who, if he be popular, has to make heavy demands on his vitality.

Care of Breeding Dogs

One who places a dog at public stud assumes certain responsibilities—the keeping of his dog in perfect health and attending most carefully to visiting matrons. The stud dog should have plenty of exercise, all the water he wants, and an abundance of good food. Raw lean meat, chopped fine or run through a mechanical grinder, makes a fine supplementary diet, and raw eggs and a little sherry can be added to this, if he becomes at all run down.

Visiting bitches must be guarded against all possible chance of a misalliance. When they arrive, they should be given a run and a drink, but do not feed them till they have quieted down a little from the excitement of the trip. If nervous, they should be kept far off from the other kennel inmates, for quiet is something to be greatly desired for them. The Golden Rule covers the care of these visitors like a blanket—just treat them as you would have a bitch of your own treated under the same circumstances.

When a bitch has returned to her home kennels, she should take the rest cure a day or so. After that, for a month or six weeks she need be treated no differently from any of her kennel mates, save to see that she has plenty to eat and that her stomach and bowels are in perfect order.

When she begins to show signs of heavy whelp take her away from the others, and while her exercise ought to be kept up by long walks, she should not be allowed to run or romp, or she may miscarry. Her box should be fixed a few days before the pups are to be born. Let it be large enough for her to stretch out in, but not big enough to give her room in which to move about, or she may kill or injure the pups by treading on them.

Once in a while, one has a bitch who neglects her pups disgracefully, but the usual thing, in terriers at least, is over attention to the sacrifice of her own condition. A few bitches eat their newborn pups. Fear is the motive, but once done they seem to get the habit. Feeding quantities of raw meat just before they are to whelp is the best, but not a sure cure. Bad mothers, ones who walk on their babies, neglect them, or turn cannibal, are very rare among the terriers.

To return to the box; it should, as I have said, be just large enough to be comfortable. The best bedding for the whelping time is a bit of old carpet, to be substituted by straw when the family has safely arrived. A little shelf, about two inches wide and tacked round the box three inches from the bottom, will prove to be good puppy life insurance, for it keeps them from being pressed to death against the sides of the nest.

Terriers whelp better if left to themselves. It is the rarest thing for them to have any trouble, and if one will just keep a weather eye open to see that things are really going well, they will continue to do so without interference. The pups should be born inside two hour intervals, and if this limit be passed the mother needs attention. The drugs used, however, are so strong and so poisonous and an operation is so delicate that it is invariably better to call in the veterinarian's skilled aid.

PUPPIES

After the puppies are all born, the mother should be given a bowl of thin oatmeal gruel and left alone. She will ordinarily clean up the nest herself, eating the after-births and licking the puppies clean. I have found that after she has cleaned a pup, which she does as soon as it is born, it is advisable to take it from her, wrap it in flannel to keep it warm and dry, and to wash off the navel cord with some mild disinfectant such as listerine, or a very dilute solution of bichloride of mercury or carbolic acid. Cold is fatal to very young puppies, and the navel cord is the source of a germ infection that kills many in the nest.

The dam, while nursing her family, must have an abundance of food—plenty of soups, gruel, meats, and milk, but not many vegetables, for they are full of water and waste. She needs more concentrated nourishment. When you think that you can fairly "see puppies grow," you can appreciate how great a drain there is on the mother. Because of this, it is never advisable to let a terrier attempt to raise at the outside, more than five puppies, and four is really better than five. If a foster cannot be obtained—very often the local Pound will have a healthy mongrel, which they will let you have for the license fee—it is kindness and economy to kill off the puppies in excess of four or five.

Which ones to destroy is a delicate question. It is usually safe to discard the last one born, since he is so often the runt of the family that he is known to kennel men and veterinarians as the " wreckling." It takes a very experienced eye to tell much about the points of a new-born puppy, but two salient features to be remembered are that not once in a hundred times will a light eye get darker; and any tendency to big ears is comparatively easy to spot and invariably gets worse. A good safe rule in terrier puppies is to save the ones with the longest, flattest heads, the heaviest, straightest forelegs; dark eyes, small ears, short bodies, taking these points in the order named, but discarding any puppy who is glaringly off in any of these details.

The mother will wean the pups herself when they begin to grow their teeth, and it is best to leave this to nature. When their eyes are opened, they should be taught to drink for themselves by sticking their noses into a saucer of sweetened milk. About the time they are fully weaned, they should be treated for worms. After this first worming, they should have similar treatment every six weeks till they are six months old, and twice more after that before they are out of the puppy class. All dogs should be treated for worms twice a year as long as they live.

Growing Pups

Growing pups need three things—food, room, and sunlight. When first weaned, they should be fed milk, gruels, and soups five times a day and the number of meals gradually lessened and the amount of solid foods gradually increased, till at a year old, they are fed the same as their older kennel companions. The more room puppies have, the better they are. This is probably the reason that the ones farmed out always do so much better than those kennel raised. They may get all sorts of food and they certainly do not get the attention given the ones in the kennels, but a farm-raised youngster is always healthier, bigger, and stronger.

Sunlight acts on puppies as it does on growing plants. Winter pups are proverbially more troublesome than those born in the spring. Most fanciers, therefore, see to it that their brood bitches whelp only in the spring. One litter a year is enough to ask for any terrier.

Small Kennels

In conclusion, a word to the small kennel owner. He is apt to think things are unfairly distributed and that he has not the chance either in the show ring, the field, or the breeding kennel that the large owner has. In the field, and especially in the breeding kennel, he really has an advantage. It is well known that the greatest number of good dogs are bred by owners of from one to five bitches, for they study their needs more carefully and can give the puppies better attention. Let the small breeder but study his breed; know its past great dogs; understand the meaning of pedigrees; mate his bitches according to his knowledge; rear his puppies carefully, and he will turn out better home breds than those from the big kennels.

SHOWS AND SHOW DOGS

CHAPTER VIII

SHOWS AND SHOW DOGS

THE Britisher's inborn love of sport, dogs, and breeding invented the dog show, but not so very long ago, for even in England, bench shows, as a recognized institution, are only a little over half a century old. Their fame and popularity have, however, circled the globe.

The English fancier can truthfully boast that there are more thoroughbred dogs to the mile in Great Britain than to fifty miles in any other country, and one is not surprised to find that there are more bench shows held there in a week than in a month in the United States. We, on this side of the ocean, are their nearest rivals, for while European countries have taken up the dog and his showing, still they are as much behind us as we are behind " the tight little isle."

Continental fanciers have a great deal to learn about dogs, and from their very dispositions it is doubtful if, with the possible exception of the serious, hard-working, painstaking Germans, they will ever become truly doggy. In the first place, they count their pennies very carefully when buying a dog; and in the second place, they are not really fanciers at heart, but have merely taken up dogs as a fashionable whim.

Show Rules

The first American shows were run in a haphazard, friendly, go-as-you-please way, but it very soon became evident that some governing body was as much a necessity in dogdom, as on the race track, in college athletics, or among yachtsmen. Accordingly, the American Kennel Club grew up naturally to fill this place. In form the A. K. C., as it is called, is a congress. Its members are not individuals, but clubs, which are represented by regularly elected delegates at the meetings of the parent organization. These clubs are of two types; the local clubs, composed of the fanciers of a certain city or district, and the specialty clubs, whose members are the fanciers the country over devoted to one particular breed.

The local clubs, like the Westminster Kennel Club of New York City or the Philadelphia Dog Show Association, are organized primarily for the giving of bench shows. The specialty clubs, of which the Fox Terrier Club of America is an example, are devoted primarily to fostering the interests of their breed. This they do by offering special prizes, by seeing that competent judges officiate, and by holding shows where only dogs of their breed are exhibited.

All shows, whether given by local or specialty associations, are held under A. K. C. rules. The regulation of these shows is the principal work done at the club's offices at 1 Liberty Street, New York. The A. K. C., however, does more than this. It publishes annually the dog Stud Book, and the A. K. C. *Gazette*, a semi-monthly, official journal. Moreover, the Club is judicial as well as legislative and executive in its functions, and tries the offenders of the kennel world. Last, but not least, it has jurisdiction over field trials, both for bird dogs and hounds.

The A. K. C. recognizes as thoroughbred dogs seventy-seven distinct breeds—not counting several subdivisions of breeds into varieties based on coats or colors. Any dog of any recognized breed may be entered in the Stud Book, provided it has three generations of pure-blood pedigree. The registration fee is one dollar and includes the assigning of an official number to the dog, entry in the Stud Book for that year, a certificate of his registration, and the right, throughout the life of the dog, to show him, regardless of ownership, at any A. K. C. show. Unregistered dogs have to be "listed" for each show they attend, and for this a fee of twenty-five cents is always charged.

Classes and Prizes

The usual classes at a bench show are the puppy, novice, limit, open, and winners', and in the more popular breeds these are divided by sex. The puppy class is for any dog between the ages of six months and one year, but, of course, none can be entered whose date and place of birth, sire, dam, and breeder are unknown. The novice class is for dogs bred in the United States, Canada, Mexico, or Cuba who have never won a first prize (wins in the puppy class being excepted). The limit class is for dogs who have not won six first prizes in that class, but dogs who have won their championship are barred. Any dog over six months of age may be shown in the open class.

If any three of the above classes are given at a show, a winners' class is always added. There is no entry fee for this class, but in it the winners of the other classes meet and are

SHOWS AND SHOW DOGS

judged. At different shows various other classes are sometimes given, as a junior class for dogs between six and eighteen months, a class for champions, and many divisions are made according to weight and color in different breeds.

It is by wins in the winners' class that a dog secures the right to prefix to his name the honorable and much coveted title of "Champion." To win this, the dog must get fifteen points. Every win in the winners' class counts a certain number of points, according to the number of dogs actually on the bench at the show: 1000 dogs or over, five points; 750 dogs or over, four points; 500 dogs or over, three points; 250 dogs or over, two points; under 250 dogs, one point. Specialty shows, devoted to one breed, count five points. Fifteen of these points, provided three of them have been won at one show and at least three different judges have awarded the dog first in the winners' class, make a dog a champion. The A. K. C. gives a championship certificate to the owner, who can also buy a championship medal for three dollars, if his dog is registered.

QUALIFICATIONS FOR ENTRY

Novices are cautioned to read most carefully the rules published in the premium lists of all

A. K. C. dog shows before they fill out their entry blanks and to exercise great care in doing this, for mistakes are on their own heads. Their dog may be disqualified and his wins canceled should they fail to fill in the necessary particulars correctly. In case of any attempt at fraud, they will be themselves disqualified, which is a doggy ex-communication. Disqualified persons are not only barred from judging, showing, or registering, but dogs owned or bred by them during their term of disqualification cannot be shown or registered.

No dog that is lame (except temporarily), blind, castrated, spayed, deaf, dyed, or in any way "faked" can be shown, and all entries are examined by a registered veterinarian when they first come to the show. They must be passed by him, as sound and free from contagious disease, before they will be accepted. Every dog must be the *bona fide* property of the exhibitor. These, and the other simple rules are easy to understand, and intent to deceive can be the only reason for their neglect or misunderstanding.

PREPARATION FOR SHOWING

To show a dog at his best, in the very pink of perfect condition, is the only way to insure that he will be placed by the judge where he deserves. Many a dog, really better than his rival in the ring, has gone down because of condition, and defeat is not only unpleasant, but also a great handicap to a show dog. Perfect health, no fat, well-developed muscles—these are the foundation of a terrier's "fitness."

A little change in diet or exercise is the best and the easiest way to accomplish this physical perfection. Tonics and pills and powders, "conditioners," as they are called, are not all they are cracked up to be. It is like doping a race-horse, or a pugilist. It works for a time, but the end is inevitable and always the same.

A terrier is easy to get "fit," and the only thing that may cause the exhibitor loss of sleep is the condition of a wire coat. Wire coats are—there is no use fishing about for any excuse—wire coats are a bother. A great, big three-quarters of the trouble is overcome, however, if the dog has been carefully and regularly groomed. Such a dog does not need much trimming—mainly a little cleaning up about the head and legs. On the other hand, one who has been neglected needs the services of a skilled canine tonsorial artist to put him down before the judge with a coat that meets the requirements of the ring.

The A. K. C. permits plucking and pulling with the fingers and brushing and combing as much as you wish, but the use of knives, razors, scissors, or clippers is strictly tabooed. It is too bad that the trimming of wire terriers is carried so far as is the style to-day. Even though legalized by the A. K. C., it so alters a dog and so improves a bad coat that it savors pretty strongly of faking. There is, however, little chance of there being any immediate reform, and to show successfully, one must obey the dictates of Mistress Fashion.

Handling in the Ring

A dog in perfect condition, with his coat trimmed in the approved style, may yet fail to get his deserts in the show ring, if not properly handled. The professional handlers are past masters at the art of making a dog appear at his very best in the ring, and a great deal of their success is due to this skill. The cry about the partiality of judges to professionally shown dogs has been often heard, but to one who watches a class actually being shown on the sawdust, there seems little grounds for complaint. The mental state of the man who can realize the better showing of the dogs handled by the paid professionals in every ring but his own appeals to the sense of humor of a close and impartial observer.

The novice cannot do better than to steal a leaf out of the book of the professional handlers. By a careful study of their methods he can learn to show his own dogs so that they will always be at their best. He will make their strongest points apparent and hide their weakness, at the same time seeing to it religiously that they catch the judicial eye.

It is well to take a puppy destined for a show career and teach him to show. It is just as easy to teach him to stand firm on his pins, all alert, full of fire, yet not bobbing about like a jumping-jack, as it is to have him sit up and beg, or to "play dead." To a "public dog" it is an infinitely more useful accomplishment.

A little bit of boiled liver, the sweetest tit-bit on a dog's menu, is an excellent thing to carry into the ring with you, but it is a grave mistake to be forever teasing and nagging at your entry. Leave him alone as much as possible. Do not wear out his spirits and your own patience, but just see that he is kept awake, standing firm so as to show his front to advantage, and so placed that the judge looks at him from the most advantageous position. If he has a poor colored eye, keep his tail pointed at the source of the light; if his back is plenty long, do not let the judge see more of his profile than possible, and so on, with different rules for each dog in the world.

Bad manners in the ring are the poorest of poor sportsmanship. Never try to hide another's dog and do not let your dog pick at, or worry another entry. The terriers are all inclined to "start things" in the ring anyway, and each exhibitor ought to do his best to prevent the ring from becoming a whirling, barking, tugging bedlam. No judge can do his best under such disconcerting conditions, and he has a hard enough time at best, so exhibitors ought to help him as much as they are able.

Very, very seldom does one meet an exhibitor who will come out frankly and say that he was beaten fairly, even if he has shown a regular "rotter" against an "out-and-outer." It does not cost one single, red cent to congratulate the owner of the dog who has beaten yours. If he has done so fairly, it is but the decent thing to do, and if you think your dog is the better, why you have the consolation of knowing that there is going to be another show where another judge will hand out the ribbons probably the very next week. It is also a mighty nice thing to find a good point or two to mention in the dogs that have been placed behind yours, assuming, of course, that you have not had the fate of being "given the gate."

These little courtesies of the ring are often sadly lacking at our American shows. Fanciers have a world of things in common and, instead of bitterest rivals, they should be the best of friends. Friendly rivalry adds ninety per cent to the pleasures of being a fancier, and in this a man gets just about what he gives.

Shipping and Benching

In sending a dog to a show, even if the distance be short and you are going along, it is best to crate him. It costs a little more, but many an unboxed dog has been lost or injured, and the railroads assume absolutely no responsibility in these cases. The express companies do charge a very high rate (one and a half times that charged for merchandise) for very poor service, but they are at least responsible for dogs committed to their charge. In England, wicker hampers are very popular for shipping dogs, but here, while lightness is to be sought, they are hardly strong enough to withstand the gentle care of our "baggage heavers."

The shows provide bedding, food, and water, but the fancier supplies his own chains and leads. To fasten a dog on the exhibition bench, bench chains, as they are called, are used. These are either nickel or brass in finish, with snaps at both ends. By means of them a dog can be so fastened that he can move about comfortably and yet not hang himself by falling over the front or get into trouble with his neighbors beyond the partitions.

In the show ring, however, these chains would be too heavy, and it is the custom to show terriers on long leather leads. There are two styles in vogue. One is a regular lead fastened with a snap to the ordinary collar, which should be a half-inch strap of plain leather. The other is the slip collar, or a long lead with a loop at one or both ends. The loop is slipped over the dog's head and fastened by a sliding clasp. All leads and collars for terriers should be light and plain. Fancy, studded collars with bells and ribbons look about as well on a terrier as diamonds on a bellboy.

The showing of dogs is rapidly becoming one of our most popular sports. The number of shows increases wonderfully each year, and every season the entries become more and more numerous. Daily, there are recruits enlisting in the army of dog fanciers. There is no denying the potency of the charm woven by the dog show. The confirmed fancier fairly loves the barking roar of the benched dogs; that peculiarly distinctive smell—a strange mixture of dog, disinfectant, and sawdust; the excitement of the ring; the doggy parties at lunches, dinners and at night after the show is over. It is all very different from anything else in the world of sport, this charm of the bench show. It is sure to hold in a fast grip any dog lover who falls under its sway.

THE END

OUTING
HANDBOOKS *The new textbooks for outdoor work and play*

℃. Each book deals with a separate subject and deals with it thoroughly. If you want to know anything about Airedales an OUTING HANDBOOK gives you all you want. If it's Apple Growing, another OUTING HANDBOOK meets your need. The Fisherman, the Camper, the Poultry-raiser, the Automobilist, the Horseman, all varieties of outdoor enthusiasts, will find separate volumes for their separate interests. There is no waste space.

℃. The series is based on the plan of one subject to a book and each book complete. The authors are experts. Each book has been specially prepared for this series and all are published in uniform style, flexible cloth binding.

℃. Two hundred titles are projected. The series covers all phases of outdoor life, from bee-keeping to big-game shooting. Among the books now ready or in preparation are those described on the following pages.

OUTING PUBLISHING COMPANY
OUTING MAGAZINE   *Yachting*   OUTING HANDBOOKS
141-145 WEST 36TH ST NEW YORK   122 S. MICHIGAN AVE. CHICAGO

THE AIREDALE, by Williams Haynes. The book opens with a short chapter on the origin and development of the Airedale, as a distinctive breed. The author then takes up the problems of type as bearing on the selection of the dog, breeding, training and use. The book is designed for the non-professional dog fancier, who wishes common sense advice which does not involve elaborate preparation or expenditure. Chapters are included on the care of the dog in the kennel and simple remedies for ordinary diseases.

"It ought to be read and studied by every Airedale owner and admirer."—Howard Keeler, Airedale Farm Kennels.

APPLE GROWING, by M. C. Burritt. The various problems confronting the apple grower, from the preparation of the soil and the planting of the trees to the marketing of the fruit, are discussed in detail by the author. Chapter headings are:— The Outlook for the Growing of Apples—Planning for the Orchard—Planting and Growing the Orchard—Pruning the Trees—Cultivation and Cover Cropping—Manuring and Fertilizing—Insects and Diseases Affecting the Apple—The Principles and Practice of Spraying—Harvesting and Storing—Markets and Marketing—Some Hints on Renovating Old Orchards—The Cost of Growing Apples.

THE AUTOMOBILE—Its Selection, Care and Use, by Robert Sloss. This is a plain, practical discussion of the things that every man needs to know if he is to buy the right car and get the most out of it. The various details of operation and care are given in simple, intelligent terms. From it the car owner can easily learn the mechanism of his motor and the art of locating motor trouble, as well as how to use his car for the greatest pleasure. A chapter is included on building garages.

BACKWOODS SURGERY AND MEDICINE, by Charles S. Moody, M. D. A handy book for the prudent lover of the woods who doesn't expect to be ill but believes in being on the safe side. Common-sense methods for the treatment of the ordinary wounds and accidents are described—setting a broken limb, reducing a dislocation, caring for burns, cuts, etc. Practical remedies for camp diseases are recommended, as well as the ordinary indications of the most probable ailments. Includes a list of the necessary medical and surgical supplies.

The manager of a mine in Nome, Alaska, writes as follows: "I have been on the trail for years (twelve in the Klondike and Alaska) and have always wanted just such a book as Dr. Moody's Backwoods Surgery and Medicine."

THE BULL TERRIER, by Williams Haynes. This is a companion book to "The Airedale" and "Scottish and Irish Terriers" by the same author. Its greatest usefulness is as a guide to the dog owner who wishes to be his own kennel manager. A full account of the development of the breed is given as also description of best types and standards. Recommendations for the care of the dog in health or sickness are included. The chapter heads cover such matters as:—The Bull Terrier's History—Training the Bull Terrier—The Terrier in Health—Kennelling—Diseases.

CAMP COOKERY, by Horace Kephart. "The less a man carries in his pack the more he must carry in his head", says Mr. Kephart. This book tells what a man should carry in both pack and head. Every step is traced—the selection of provisions and utensils, with the kind and quantity of each, the preparation of game, the building of fires, the cooking of every conceivable kind of food that the camp outfit or woods, fields or streams may provide—even to the making of desserts. Every recipe is the result of hard practice and long experience. Every recipe has been carefully tested. It is the book for the man who wants to dine well and wholesomely, but

in true wilderness fashion without reliance on grocery stores or elaborate camp outfits. It is adapted equally well to the trips of every length and to all conditions of climate, season or country; the best possible companion for one who wants to travel light and live well. The chapter headings tell their own story. Provisions—Utensils—Fires—Dressing and Keeping Game and Fish—Meat—Game—Fish and Shell Fish—Cured Meats, etc.—Eggs—Breadstuffs and Cereals—Vegetables—Soups—Beverages and Desserts.

> "*Camp Cookery is destined to be in the kit of every tent dweller in the country.*"—*Edwin Markham in the San Francisco Examiner.*

CANOE AND BOAT BUILDING, by Victor Slocum. All of us like to think we could build a boat if we had to. Mr. Slocum tells us how to do it. Designs are given for the various types of canoes as well as full descriptions for preparing the material and putting it together. Small dories and lapstreak boats are also included.

CATTLE DISEASES, by B. T. Woodward. Mr. Woodward takes up in detail the various common diseases to which cattle are liable. His book is designed for the aid of the practical farmer in cases where the skilled veterinarian is not necessary. A careful description of the various diseases is given and the accepted forms of treatment stated.

EXERCISE AND HEALTH, by Dr. Woods Hutchinson. Dr. Hutchinson takes the common-sense view that the greatest problem in exercise for most of us is to get enough of the right kind. The greatest error in exercise is not to take enough, and the greatest danger in athletics is in giving them up. The Chapter heads are illuminating. Errors in Exercise—Exercise and the Heart—Muscle Maketh Man—The Danger of Stopping Athletics—Exercise that Rests. It is written in a direct matter-of-fact manner with an avoidance of medical terms, and a strong emphasis on the rational, all-round manner of living that is best calculated to bring a man to a ripe old age with little illness or consciousness of bodily weakness.

"One of the most readable books ever written on physical exercise."—Luther H. Gulick, M.D., Department of Child Hygiene, Russell Sage Foundation.

FARM DRAINAGE & IRRIGATION, by W. J. McGee. Sometimes it is necessary to spend money to get water on the land; sometimes to get it off. Mr. McGee has studied the question from both angles in his work for the Department of Agriculture and this book will contain his latest and fullest conclusions. Particular attention will be paid to the matter of sub-surface irrigation to which little heed has been given until lately.

FENCING, by Edward Breck. Dr. Breck was for many years one of the best-known amateur fencers in America and is acquainted with the best swordsmen of the present day, here and abroad. His book is a practical guide for those who wish to know the most approved practice in the use of the foil, duelling sword, or saber. Suggestions are given on training and condition, as well as on the finer points of the game.

THE FINE ART OF FISHING, by Samuel G. Camp.
Combines the pleasure of catching fish with the gratification of following the sport in the most approved manner. The suggestions offered are helpful to beginner and expert anglers. The range of fish and fishing conditions covered is wide and includes such subjects as "Casting Fine and Far Off", "Strip-Casting for Bass", "Fishing for Mountain Trout" and "Autumn Fishing for Lake Trout". The book is pervaded with a spirit of love for the streamside and the out-doors generally which the genuine angler will appreciate. A companion book to "Fishing Kits and Equipment". The advice on outfitting so capably given in that book is supplemented in this later work by equally valuable information on how to use the equipment.
 "*Will encourage the beginner and give pleasure to the expert fisherman.*"—*N. Y. Sun.*

FISHING KITS AND EQUIPMENT by Samuel G. Camp. A complete guide to the angler buying a new outfit. Every detail of the fishing kit of the freshwater angler is described, from rod-tip to creel, and clothing. Special emphasis is laid on outfitting for

fly fishing, but full instruction is also given to the man who wants to catch pickerel, pike, muskellunge, lake-trout, bass and other freshwater game fishes. Prices are quoted for all articles recommended and the approved method of selecting and testing the various rods, lines, leaders, etc., is described.
 "*A complete guide to the angler buying a new outfit.*"—
 —*Peoria Herald.*

FISHING WITH FLOATING FLIES by Samuel G. Camp. This is an art that is comparatively new in this country although English anglers have used the dry fly for generations. Mr. Camp has given the matter special study and is one of the few American anglers who really understands the matter from the selection of the outfit to the landing of the fish. His book takes up the process in that order, namely—How to Outfit for Dry Fly Fishing—How, Where, and When to Cast—The Selection and Use of Floating Flies—Dry Fly Fishing for Brook, Brown and Rainbow Trout—Hooking, Playing and Landing—Practical Hints on Dry Fly Fishing.

THE FOX TERRIER, by Williams Haynes. As in his other books on the terrier, Mr. Haynes takes up the origin and history of the breed, its types and standards, and the more exclusive representatives down to the present time. Training the Fox Terrier—His Care and Kenneling in Sickness and Health—and the Various Uses to Which He Can be Put—are among the phases handled.

THE GASOLINE MOTOR, by Harold Whiting Slauson. Deals with the practical problems of motor operation. The standpoint is that of the man who wishes to know how and why gasoline generates power and something about the various types. Describes in detail the different parts of motors and the faults to which they are liable. Also gives full directions as to repair and upkeep. Various chapters deal with Types of Motors—Valves—Bearings—Ignition—Carburetors—Lubrication—Fuel—Two Cycle Motors.

GUNSMITHING FOR THE AMATEUR, by Edward C. Crossman. Mr. Crossman, who is one of the best-known rifle experts in the country, takes up in detail the care and repair of the gun. He discusses such questions as The Present Development of the Gun—Tools for the Amateur—Rifle Barrels—Smooth Bore Barrels—Rifle Actions—Pistol and Gun Actions—Refinishing and Processing—The Stock, Sights and Aids to Accuracy.

David Buffum. Mr. Buffum takes up the common, every-day problems of the ordinary horse-user, such as feeding, shoeing, simple home remedies, breaking and the cure for various equine vices. An important chapter is that tracing the influx of Arabian blood into the English and American horses and its value and limitations. Chapters are included on draft-horses, carriage horses, and the development of the two-minute trotter. It is distinctly a sensible book for the sensible man who wishes to know how he can improve his horses and his horsemanship at the same time.

INTENSIVE FARMING, by L. C. Corbett. A discussion of the meaning, method and value of intensive methods in agriculture. This book is designed for the convenience of practical farmers who find themselves under the necessity of making a living out of high-priced land.

LAYING OUT THE FARM FOR PROFIT, by L. G. Dodge. One of the farmers' great problems is to put every acre of his land to the best possible use. This book discusses the methods of obtaining this result. The author is an investigator for the Department of Agriculture and has given particular attention to this subject.

THE MOTOR BOAT--Its Selection, Care and Use, by H. W. Slauson. The intending purchaser is advised as to the type of motor boat best suited to his particular needs and how to keep it in running condition after purchased. The Chapter headings are: Kinds and Uses of Motor Boats—When the Motor Balks—Speeding of the Motor Boat—Getting More Power from a New Motor—How to Install a Marine Power Plant—Accessories—Covers, Canopies and Tops—Camping and Cruising—The Boathouse.

NAVIGATION FOR THE AMATEUR, by Capt. E. T. Morton. A short treatise on the simpler methods of finding position at sea by the observation of the sun's altitude and the use of the sextant and chronometer. It is arranged especially for yachtsmen and amateurs who wish to know the simpler formulae for the necessary navigation involved in taking a boat anywhere off shore. Illustrated with drawings. Chapter headings: Fundamental Terms—Time—The Sumner Line—The Day's Work, Equal Altitude, and Ex-Meridian Sights—Hints on Taking Observations.

OUTDOOR PHOTOGRAPHY, by Julian A. Dimock. A solution of all the problems in camera work out-of-doors. The various subjects dealt with are The Camera—Lens and Plates—Light and Exposure — Development — Prints and Printing — Composition — Landscapes — Figure Work — Speed Photography — The Leaping Tarpon—Sea Pictures—In the Good Old Winter Time—Wild Life. The purpose of the book is to serve as a guide not only for the man or woman who has just taken up the use of the camera, but also for those who have progressed far enough to know some of the problems that confront them.

OUTDOOR SIGNALLING, by Elbert Wells. Mr. Wells has perfected a method of signalling by means of wig-wag, light, smoke, or whistle which is as simple as it is effective. The fundamental principle can be learnt in ten minutes and its application is far easier than that of any other code now in use. It permits also the use of cipher and can be adapted to almost any imaginable conditions of weather, light, or topography.

"I find it to be the simplest and most practical book on signalling published."—Frank H. Schrenk, Director of Camp Belgrade.

"One of the finest things of the kind I have ever seen. I believe my seven year old boy can learn to use this system, and I know that we will find it very useful here in our Boy Scout work."—Lyman G. Haskell, Physical Director, Y. M. C. A., Jacksonville, Fla.

PACKING AND PORTAGING, by Dillon Wallace. Mr. Wallace has brought together in one volume all the valuable information on the different ways of making and carrying the different kinds of packs. The ground covered ranges from man-packing to horse-packing, from the use of the tump line to throwing the diamond hitch. The various chapters deal with Packing and the Outfit—The Canoe and Its Equipment—Camp Equipment for the Canoe Trip—Personal Equipment—Food—The Portage—Travel with Saddle and Pack Animals—Saddle and Pack Equipment—Adjusting the Pack—Some Practical Hitches—Traveling Without a Pack Horse—Afoot in Summer—With Snowshoes and Toboggan—With Dogs and Komatik.

PRACTICAL POULTRY KEEPING, by R. B. Sando. In effect a comprehensive manual for the instruction of the man who desires to begin poultry raising on a large or small scale and to avoid the ordinary mistakes to which the beginner is prone. All the statements are based on the author's own experience, and special care has been taken to avoid sensationalism and exaggeration. The general contents are Poultry Keeping and Keepers—Housing and Yarding—Fixtures and Equipment—Choosing and Buying Stock—Foods and Feeding—Hatching and Raising Chicks—Poultry Diseases. Illustrated.

PROFITABLE BREEDS OF POULTRY, by Arthur S. Wheeler. Mr. Wheeler discusses from personal experience the best-known general purpose breeds. Advice is given from the standpoint of the man who desires results in eggs and stock rather than in specimens for exhibition. In addition to a careful analysis of stock—good and bad—and some conclusions regarding housing and management, the author writes in detail regarding Plymouth Rocks, Wyandottes, Orpingtons, Rhode Island Reds, Mediterraneans and the Cornish.

"This is an invaluable book for those who would make a success in the poultry business."—Grand Rapids, (Mich.) Herald.

RIFLES AND RIFLE SHOOTING, by Charles Askins. A practical manual describing various makes and mechanisms, in addition to discussing in detail the range and limitations in the use of the rifle. Among other things, the chapters deal with The Development of the American Breech-Loading Rifle—Single Shot Rifle—Lever-Action Repeater—Pump-Action Repeater and

Military Bolt-Action—Double Rifle—Rifle and Shotgun—Self-Loading Rifle—Rifle Cartridges, Miniature and Gallery—Small Game—Match-Rifle Cartridges and Their Manipulation—High Power, Small Bore Hunting Cartridges—Big Bore, High Power Cartridges—Trajectory, Accuracy, and Power of Hunting Cartridges—Weight of Rifle and Recoil—Stocks and Triggers—Rifle Sights—Positions for Rifle Shooting—Outdoor Target Shooting,—Quick Firing and Running Shots—Fancy Snap and Wingshooting—Two-Hundred Yard Sharpshooting.

SCOTTISH AND IRISH TERRIERS, by Williams Haynes. This is a companion book to "The Airedale", and deals with the history and development of both breeds. For the owner of the dog, valuable information is given as to the use of the terriers, their treatment in health, their treatment when sick, the principles of dog breeding, and dog shows and rules.

"The happy owner of a terrier for the first time could not go wrong if he follows Mr. Haynes' advice."— Brooklyn Standard Union.

CPSIA information can be obtained
at www.ICGtesting.com
Printed in the USA
LVHW082021201021
700968LV00002B/152